Core 2017

D0408735

Butter

BAKED GOODS

Rosie Daykin

BAKED GOODS

Nostalgic Recipes from a
Little Neighborhood Bakery

PHOTOGRAPHY BY
JANIS NICOLAY

appetite
by RANDOM HOUSE

Appetite by Random House and colophon are registered trademarks of
Random House of Canada Limited

Library and Archives of Canada Cataloguing in Publication is available upon request

ISBN: 978-0-449-01583-4

Cover and book design: Kelly Hill
Cover and author photograph: Janis Nicolay
Printed and bound in China

Published by Appetite by Random House,
a division of Random House of Canada Limited

www.randomhouse.ca

10 9 8 7 6 5 4 3 2

To Paul and India,
my mostly companions.
You are my home,
my love, my life.

Contents

Butter

Hours of Enjoyment
Tuesday - Saturday
10:30am to 5:30pm
604-221-4322

Have you ever wondered what your personal theme song would be if you had one? I remember the day my husband, Paul, introduced me to mine, a wonderful song by Guy Clark called "The Cape." The chorus goes something like: "Life is just a leap of faith, spread your arms, hold your breath, and always trust your cape." Paul felt this summed me up perfectly. I am not sure if this says I am bold, or fearless, or just plain nuts, but so far the cape is holding! I am known to be true to my word: If I say I am going to do something, I always do—well, almost always. Okay, sometimes I skip that exercise class or forget to sign up for Italian lessons, but the big stuff, the life-changing stuff, I follow through on. So when I was six and announced that I was one day going to own a bakery (actually, I think I said donut shop, but let's not split hairs), I already had a plan.

By six years old I was a keen baker, turning out the Six-Minute Cake (a one-bowl chocolate cake with the magic ingredient of vinegar) almost daily. I grew up in a busy household with three siblings. Our home was abuzz with family, friends and pets galore, so finding some unsuspecting victim to feed my creations to wasn't much of a challenge. Fortunately, my baking skills improved dramatically with all that practice and I eventually mastered a wide range of cookies, cakes, bars and pies. I loved nothing more than being in the kitchen, surrounded by bowls and beaters covered in the remnants of batter, waiting—impatiently—for the moment I could pull something warm and delicious from the oven.

Chocolate cake
1 1/2 c. flour
1 c. sugar
1/4 c. cocoa.
1 tsp. baking powder
1 tsp. soda
1/2 tsp. salt

1 tbsp. vinegar
1 tsp. vanilla
1/3 c. oil
1 c. warm water

350°
35 m

Life carried on and I grew older. Paul and I met, fell madly in love and were married in 1989. Three years later I gave birth to our daughter, the lovely Miss India Rose. Life was hectic, working and raising a child, but I could always find solace in the kitchen. I had by then become quite a successful interior designer, but I still found myself daydreaming of the day I could make a living baking cakes and cookies to my heart's content. It is hard to express (but, I think, simple enough to understand) the immense happiness I get when just the act of sharing something I enjoy brings someone else the same happiness. I couldn't imagine a more satisfying way to spend my day.

As with most things in my life, opening Butter Baked Goods was all about timing and my well-honed gut feeling. I saw the need in the marketplace for what I was creating at home: simple homemade treats with no additives or preservatives. Nothing all tricked up, just real food like I remembered as a child. I knew of nowhere in my city to purchase a classic chocolate layer cake piled high with butter cream and multi-colored sprinkles, a cake just waiting for birthday candles and a scoop of vanilla ice cream. And I just knew that if I was looking for it, others would be too. I was aware of how much time, attention and energy this new venture would take. (Actually, I thought I knew, but I was way off. It took so much more.) I had spent a lifetime planning the bakery inside my head, and one morning I woke and knew the time had come. Fortunately, I had the support of my family and friends, who were all there to help me breathe life into my dream. If the Amish have barn raisings, well, this was a bakery raising. And so Butter Baked Goods was born.

I came up with the name for Butter before the bakery was a reality. I love the creative process of naming things. A name can tell you so much about a person or place and, if chosen with care, I think it can help form the very person or place it represents. When Paul and I were choosing names for our soon-to-be-born baby I was confident a little girl was headed our way. When I envisioned a woman named India Rose I had this picture in my head of a woman in the 1930s standing next to her plane, goggles on and ready to fly. This woman was someone bold and fearless, yet feminine and funny. Today my India Rose is all those things and more. The name for Butter came to me just as clearly. For me, it represents something real, pure and honest. With that one word you know what we are all about. It speaks of a quality of baking that many of us grew up with, and of our nostalgia for

that. And it speaks to a trust and dependability that we sometimes find ourselves searching for in this crazy world.

With my background in interior design, I had a definite vision of how Butter should feel and look to reflect the kind of baking I wanted to create. I wanted it to be comfortable and warm, a spot to chitchat with neighbors, celebrate milestones, or pick you up after a bad day. I wasn't looking for shiny and new but something a little worn and familiar. The first time I crossed the threshold of 4321 Dunbar Street, I knew I had found Butter's home. The space had been a bakery since 1923, and I'm pretty sure that that was the last time the windows had been cleaned! It was a total train wreck, so old and filthy that whenever I met someone who told me they used to shop there, I silently wondered how they had survived to tell the tale. Yet underneath it all I saw a gem. It was the screen door that did it. Original to the space, it was wide and solid and welcoming, and the first thing you touched when entering the building. It made the same wonderful sound I remembered as a kid when running into the house for dinner. That forgivable slam that says, "I'm home." It was everything I wanted Butter to be, and I was sure that the moment my customers pulled on the handle, they would feel the same way. I wanted every nook and cranny of Butter to welcome my customers and make them smile— from the pale pink ceiling and the black and white checkerboard pattern of the floor, right down to the little iron Scotty dog named Mr. Sweaters who acts as our doorstop, gatekeeper and self-appointed mascot. I made sure there was a big opening between the bakery's storefront and the kitchen so anyone who came in could see what we were up to. We didn't have any secrets, and I wanted to be able to say hello to customers as I iced cakes and rolled dough.

On September 4, 2007, Butter Baked Goods opened for business. There was a lineup down the block of eager schoolchildren and their parents, old people, young people and everyone in between. The look on my face was somewhere between panic and elation. Having prepared for several months for the opening, I now had only one night to prepare for the next day and the day after that and the day after that . . . Those first couple of months were a blur and I experienced a level of exhaustion that words cannot describe. I didn't dare sit down for fear I might not be able to get back up, but, as with all things, time worked out the kinks. I found my rhythm—and I found some great bakers to help me along the way. Our first Thanksgiving was total madness. The image of all those people squeezed into the front of the shop, ticket in hand to retrieve their pumpkin pies, is permanently etched in my memory.

Six-Minute Cake

This was my favorite cake to make as a little girl. I didn't frost it, we just ate it up as soon as we cut it from the pan.

1 ½ cups all-purpose flour

1 cup granulated sugar

⅓ cup dark cocoa

1 teaspoon baking soda

1 teaspoon baking powder

½ teaspoon salt

1 cup water

½ cup vegetable oil

1 teaspoon pure vanilla

2 tablespoons white vinegar

MAKES: 1 (9-inch cake) about 9 to 12 pieces

YOU WILL NEED: 9- × 9-inch square or 9-inch round baking pan, buttered

1. Preheat the oven to 375°F.

2. In a large bowl, sift together the dry ingredients. Add the water, oil and vanilla and whisk to combine. Add the vinegar and whisk again until combined. Pour the batter into the prepared pan.

3. Bake in the preheated oven for 20 to 25 minutes or until a wooden skewer inserted into the center comes out clean.

4. Remove from the oven and allow to cool on a wire rack.

Butter has grown in leaps and bounds over the last six years, and many crazy and exciting things have transpired. Local grocery stores became eager to stock a selection of our baked goods—which makes our customers happy when they're in search of a sandwich cookie on a day when the bakery is closed! The gourmet marshmallows we made in little batches when we first opened grew so popular that we had to find a second space to produce just them. I love the look of delight on people's faces when I tell them I have a marshmallow factory—which is usually followed by one of disappointment when I tell them Willy Wonka and his Oompa Loompas don't work there. And I am always delighted when I receive an email from a loyal customer, writing to share their excitement that they've discovered Butter's marshmallows being sold in some far corner of North America or Japan.

I am continually amazed and flattered by how, in such a short time, Butter has become part of people's lives and traditions. Our cakes and cookies and pies are right there alongside them now as they celebrate birthdays, weddings and holidays. Butter is there for the first day of school and the last day of Little League, and it is there for the good days and the not-so-good days. I think this says something. It says that this is what people were missing. It says that while the world keeps speeding up and our lives get more and more hectic, a really good nutty chocolate chip cookie is worth slowing down for. It says that life's little pleasures can be simple.

In the fall of 2012, we opened up a second bakery location—this time as the Butter Baked Goods Café at 4907 Mackenzie Street—not too far from our original spot. Just like that first year, every Thanksgiving, Christmas, Valentine's Day, Easter and Halloween is pure madness, but we manage to laugh and bake our way through it. It helps that I love all the people I work with so much. There have been as many bumps along the way as there have been successes, but, like those nasty burns from the sneaky oven door, they heal in time, leaving a faint scar to remind you and educate you as you grow. And, all in all, Butter and I have survived.

In writing this cookbook I hope to share my love of baking and all that it can mean. I hope that it becomes part of your life and traditions in the same way that Butter already has for so many people. Baking needn't be complicated or intimidating; I don't believe it should take 45 steps to make a great dessert. My recipes were not created to impress people—they were created to spoil them, to celebrate them and to comfort them when needed. Don't worry about protecting this book; the spills and notations that I hope one day mark its pages will tell a story. A story that says I did my job; I inspired you to get into the kitchen, bake for your family and friends and always trust your cape. 𝓑

Rosie

Trust me, I know here is nothing more frustrating for a keen baker than discovering that you are out of molasses when you have a hankering for a ginger cookie! Here is a list of the basic, and some more specialized, ingredients that I like to keep on hand.

In the Cupboard

BAKING SODA AND BAKING POWDER

Make sure your baking soda and baking powder are fresh. Neither is expensive, so purchase in smaller amounts and replace often. (That's the only important thing I have to say about either.)

CHOCOLATE AND COCOA POWDER

When it comes to chocolate, you get what you pay for. It is definitely one ingredient that I like to splurge on as it really reflects in the finished product. At Butter we use semisweet dark chocolate chips that are at least 60% cacao. These have a smooth finish and work well both in chip form and melted. Grocery stores are improving their chocolate offerings as customers become more knowledgeable and demanding, but if you find your local store still comes up short, you can always purchase good-quality chocolate in blocks or bars and then cut them into chunks for cookies or melting. Cocoa is available in a natural finish or Dutch-process. Of the two, Dutch-process has a lower acidity, milder flavor and a darker color. I use only Dutch-process Bensdorp cocoa at the bakery and for the recipes in this book.

COCONUT

All the coconut used in the recipes is unsweetened, except for Butter's Coconut Cake (page 154), and the Hey There, Doll Face! bars (page 120). For these I like to use sweetened fancy long shred coconut for the tastiest results.

CONDENSED MILK

Condensed milk is a wonderful old-school ingredient and the base for many a yummy treat. It is sold in cans and, unopened, keeps seemingly forever, so you should have a few cans tucked in the pantry for emergency Hey There, Doll Face! bar attacks.

FLOUR

I always have a large bag of unbleached all-purpose flour and a smaller bag of pastry flour in the cupboard. The significant difference between them is how fine they are milled and their levels of protein and the resulting gluten. Too much gluten can make a cake tough. Pastry flour, being finely milled and having a low protein content, will produce less gluten and therefore a cake with a finer and more tender crumb than one made with all-purpose flour. All the recipes in this book call for one or the other, with the exception of Butter's Coconut Cake, which uses a small amount of coconut flour. Coconut flour can be found in most grocery stores—Bob's Red Mill is a popular brand—and I like the extra depth this flour gives to the cake.

MAPLE SYRUP

When buying maple syrup, only one word is important, and that word is *pure.* I know it can be costly, but there is no substitute.

MOLASSES

Molasses has a good shelf life and is very reasonably priced, so be sure to pick some up on your next grocery shop, or you won't be able to make Shoo Fly Pie! I buy fancy molasses over blackstrap or cooking molasses as it is less bitter and I just love the word *fancy.*

PEANUT BUTTER

There are two camps when it comes to peanut butter: the natural camp and the not-so-natural camp. I am a proud member of the not-so-natural, and by this I mean I prefer a peanut butter like Skippy or Squirrel over one with a thick layer of oil floating on top. I think they are just as delicious, easier to work with and make much less of a mess when sticking a spoon in the jar to scoop up a little afternoon snack!

PISTACHIO PASTE

I consider pistachio paste a staple because I can honestly tell you that, since opening Butter, it is the one ingredient that I now feel I can't live without. I am a lover of all things pistachio, including the color of the millwork at the bakery. It has proven to be the most versatile of ingredients, and once you have iced your first pistachio chocolate cake, you will know what I am talking about. If your local gourmet shop doesn't carry pistachio paste, purchase it online through one of the many reputable baking supply companies.

SALT

I use kosher salt in all my home baking. There is nothing wrong with using table salt, but I prefer kosher salt because it has no additives and a cleaner flavor. It is also not as finely ground as table salt, which means that a single teaspoon of kosher salt contains less salt than a teaspoon of table salt. All the recipes in this book were tested using kosher salt, so if you use table salt instead, use a little less. Maldon Sea Salt Flakes are one of my favorite things to sprinkle on top of chocolate—I love the salty-sweet combination. They are fantastic sprinkled on brownies still warm from the oven or on chocolate-almond bark.

SPICES

Even though I buy spices in small amounts, I am amazed at how quickly I amass a collection of spices that I may use only once in a while. I try to do a good cleaning at least once a year and throw out any spices that haven't been used recently. That may seem wasteful given the cost of some, but if they are old and not properly sealed, they won't add much to the baking anyway. A spice cupboard with a small amount of ground cinnamon, nutmeg, cloves and ginger is an excellent start. I am also a huge fan of pumpkin pie spice, which is a combination of the four.

SUGAR

No baking cupboard is complete without granulated sugar, dark brown sugar and icing (or confectioners') sugar. Make sure to store your brown sugar in an airtight container so it doesn't dry out and become hard. When it comes to brown sugar, demerara is my first choice, as I love the rich robust flavor it imparts. I also like to have coarse sugar on hand, for sprinkling on scones, pies and certain cookies.

Nothing compares to the taste of pure vanilla, whether in pod or liquid extract form. It is a pricey staple, but it makes a world of difference to the end product. All of the recipes in this book call for vanilla extract, but if you want to take it up a notch, you should consider adding the seeds of a vanilla pod. These will not only intensify the vanilla flavor of your butter cream, marshmallow or shortbread, but all the lovely little black seeds will add a visual clue of the vanilla flavor to come. Vanilla beans should be soft and pliable when you cut them down the center and then you can use the back of the knife to scrape out the seeds. At Butter we place the deseeded pods in a jug of pure vanilla extract to further enhance its flavor. Or you could tuck them into your sugar canister to infuse the sugar with the taste of vanilla. Be sure to keep vanilla beans tightly sealed and stored in the refrigerator.

In the Refrigerator

BUTTER

I guess I should have lots to say regarding butter, given the name of my bakery, but in all honesty I don't think there is much to discuss. In my world, there is no substitution for butter, in baking or cooking or just spreading on a cracker. The only debate is over salted or unsalted. The general consensus is that unsalted butter is the better choice as it allows you to control the salt content in your baking. Also, since salt acts as a preservative, the salted butter in the supermarket cooler may not be as fresh as the unsalted variety. I use unsalted butter when baking, but if I have only salted on hand, then salted it is. I don't get too bent out of shape over it, and neither should you. If you do use salted butter in any of these recipes, just omit or reduce the amount of salt called for, depending on your taste.

EGGS

Always use large, fresh eggs in your baking. Bring them to room temperature first, as this will give them maximum volume when they are whipped and ensure more even distribution when they are blended into a batter. If you are in a rush, you can bring the eggs to room temperature faster by placing them in a bowl of warm water for about 15 minutes.

We use a lot of fruit at Butter to make our Saturday pie offerings. People want pie all year round and in Canada, the Great White North, fresh fruit isn't available all year round unless it has been flown in from some remote land (okay, California, but you get my point). Frozen fruit is a fantastic alternative and can often impart an even better flavor than fresh fruit that was picked when unripe and then flown around the world. In particular, we find we go through a lot of raspberries, blueberries, strawberries and peaches (and also rhubarb) at the bakery. And just a quick note on lemons: When a recipe calls for lemon juice or lemon zest, use a real lemon—there is no substitute for freshly squeezed lemon juice or the intense flavor and depth of pure lemon zest. I find the best way to zest a lemon is with a Microplane grater (see page 17).

MILK AND CREAM

I have only three things to say about milk, buttermilk, sour cream or heavy cream: full fat, full fat and full fat. Buttermilk is naturally lower in fat than many other milks, but there are even lower-fat options out there—don't buy them unless you are on a diet and need something to coat chicken breasts with! Please don't scrimp thinking you will save calories; you will really just be sacrificing flavor.

NUTS

When buying nuts, buy only the freshest you can find, buy only what you need and store them in the refrigerator, tightly sealed. Nuts spoil quickly and trust me when I say that spoiled nuts are nasty. I am confident you will always be able to quickly work your way through a little stash of walnuts, pecans and almonds. It is also a good thing to note that nut pieces are cheaper than whole nuts, so keep that in mind when a recipe calls for chopped nuts.

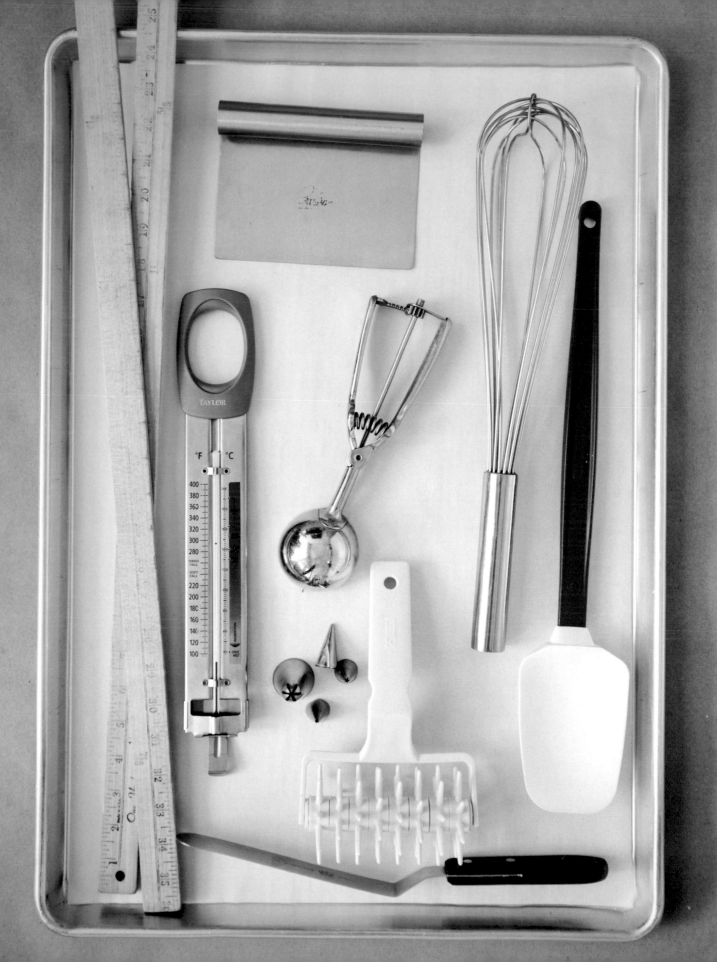

I have never been the kind of baker who has a million gadgets and gizmos for every task in the kitchen. My supplies have always been pretty limited, but they get the job done. At home I am still using the same baking sheets I bought to make cookies in my first apartment at the ripe old age of 18. I am sure new and fancier models have been developed in the years since, but I feel that my tools and I have a relationship that cannot be easily broken or replaced. Over the years, we have found a rhythm and a comfort in our work together that almost always produces successful results. Like any relationship, that comes with time and trust. I suggest buying the best you can afford, as quality tools will stand the test of time and use better than the cheaper models.

Measuring

MEASURING CUPS, JUGS AND SPOONS

You will need at least one set of good-quality measuring cups with a straight rim so you can level off the dry ingredients easily, and I tend to prefer metal over plastic. I seem to have several sets of these floating around my baking drawers, which is quite helpful when embarking on a baking bonanza. Always remember when filling dry measures that it is best to overfill them and then use a straight edge to cleanly level them off—the side of a spatula works nicely. Glass or Pyrex liquid measuring cups in 1-cup and 4-cup capacities will also come in very handy. And when buying a good set of metal measuring spoons, don't bother with those that measure all the way down to a smidge and a pinch—total nonsense.

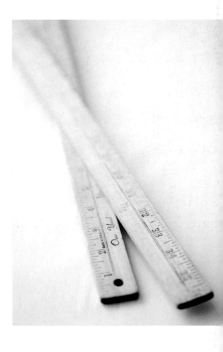

TWO BIG WOODEN YARD STICKS

Yard sticks play a big part in the kitchen at Butter, for obvious reasons and not-so-obvious reasons. First and foremost they are handy for measuring the width and length of bars before cutting them, or dividing up a roll of cinnamon buns evenly. But it is for rolling cookie dough that they are really indispensable (see page 84). You can find them at pretty much any office supply store. Look for ones that are about ¼ inch thick.

ICE CREAM SCOOPS AND MORE ICE CREAM SCOOPS

Ice cream scoops in every size will be one of the best things you ever introduce to your baking practice. Nothing helps better in achieving even distribution of batter and dough, or filling sandwich cookies and whoopie pies, not to mention creating perfect peanut butter balls. We have scoops in a variety of sizes at the bakery as we are quite specific for consistent production, but for home use, so long as you have a small, medium and large scoop on hand (with the large being a regular-sized ice cream scoop), you are set. I like using scoops with a spring-release mechanism.

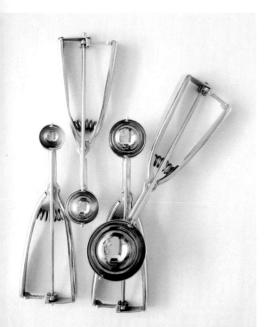

Mixing

BOWLS, BOWLS AND BOWLS

I don't know a baker who doesn't have a love of mixing bowls. I have stacks of them at home and use them continually. At Butter we use stainless-steel bowls, in a huge range of sizes, but at home I prefer ceramic or glass, even though they are heavy and not as easy to maneuver. I'm willing to put up with this because they are so darn pretty! And a small heatproof bowl really comes in useful for melting chocolate if you don't have a double boiler (see page 21).

STAND MIXER

Before opening Butter, my stand mixer was the most-used appliance in the house. I never tucked it away but displayed it proudly on the counter, ready to plug in at a moment's notice and start creating something yummy. I suggest choosing a model with the largest bowl or maximum capacity available. As with a woman's handbag, you will always manage to fill it up! A good stand mixer can be a bit of an investment, but you will have it for many years to come (I have had my KitchenAid for at least 15 years) and it is more than worth it when you consider all the work it will help you get done.

HANDHELD MIXER

A handheld mixer is an alternative to a stand mixer, and a good one will get the job done. It will, however, require a little bit more elbow grease, as it is not nearly as powerful as a stand mixer. With that in mind, make sure to purchase the best you can find, or you might find it can do little more than whip cream.

SPOONS AND WHISKS

At home I have a drawer full of spoons and whisks. At Butter we have glass canisters brimming with them. I could never have too many on hand, but for the recipes in this book a couple of large metal spoons, a simple wooden spoon and a wire balloon whisk should suffice. A stand mixer is a wonderful thing, but you will be hard-pressed to replace balloon whisks and spoons for pretty much any task.

Cutting and Zesting

COOKIE CUTTERS

We have droves of cookie cutters at Butter for every occasion you can think of, and lots of occasions you can't. I prefer copper cutters, as they are much stronger than plastic versions, and they never go rusty like some other metal options.

KNIVES

Good-quality knives are a wise and wonderful investment, but for the recipes in this book, having the following three will suffice: a large serrated knife for cutting cake layers and loaves; a large chef's knife with an 8- to 10-inch blade for cutting bars and cakes (ideally the blade should be longer than whatever you are cutting so that you can make one clean cut and avoid dragging the knife across the bars or cake); and a paring knife for trimming pastry, cutting fruit and so on.

MICROPLANE

Microplane graters are readily available at kitchen supply stores. They are much finer than standard graters and are wonderful for zesting lemons and limes. Be careful when using one because they are crazy sharp and none of these recipes call for zested fingers!

One good pair of kitchen scissors is a must, or you will find yourself hunting through the wrapping paper drawer every time you need to cut a piece of parchment.

Bakeware

BAKING SHEETS, PANS AND PIE DISHES

I have gotten through most of my baking life at home with a limited assortment of bakeware. Again, opt for the best quality you can afford, as these items can, and should, last you a lifetime. Make sure you purchase metal bakeware that has a nice heavy weight to it as they distribute the heat more evenly and will not warp or bend. Non-stick coatings are a bonus when it comes to doing the dishes! But, whether the pan has a non-stick coating or not, you should still always butter and flour it as instructed in the recipe. Here is a basic list, with quantities for each, that will cover you for almost anything in the kitchen, and definitely for all the recipes in this book:

2   11- × 17-inch rimmed cookie sheets
2   12-cup regular muffin pans
2   12-cup mini muffin pans
2   7-inch round cake pans
1   9- × 13-inch rectangular baking pan
1   8- × 8-inch square pan
1   9- × 9-inch square pan
1   9-inch tube cake pan
1   6-cup bundt pan
2   8-inch loaf pans
2   9-inch glass pie dishes
1   9-inch tart pan with removable bottom

WIRE COOLING RACKS

Having several of these in the lineup is imperative. They are useful when cooling baked goods straight out of the oven, and they also work fantastically when glazing a cake or dipping biscotti in chocolate. You can place the wire rack over a piece of parchment paper to catch all the drips.

Icing

Before opening the bakery, I had not discovered how useful a rotating cake stand can be. The height that it provides and the ease with which you can smoothly run a spatula around the sides of the cake when icing it will help give the cake a professional finish. Plus it is kind of fun to spin—like when you were little and sitting in your dad's desk chair. It also proves to be really handy when slicing a cake into layers. If you don't have a rotating cake stand, cake boards can be purchased at craft or baking supply stores in a variety of sizes. They are usually constructed of a strong stiff cardboard, coated in a gold or silver foil. Icing a cake on a cake board makes it easier to move around if you need to while you are decorating (coating the cake with coconut, nuts or chocolate sprinkles, for example). Icing the cake on either a rotating cake stand or cake board also leaves your presentation cake plate nice and clean for when you serve the cake on it.

SERRATED BLADE

A serrated or ribbed blade can be found online or at your local baking supply store. They usually have three sides with three different rib sizes, for creating various effects when icing cakes. All you require for a really nice and even finish on your cake is a steady hand and a rotating cake stand (see Icing Cakes on page 145).

PIPING BAGS AND TIPS

I cannot stress enough how much use you will get out of a couple of piping bags and a handful of piping tips. Some people might be intimidated by a piping bag, but this tool is truly a breeze to master and can give a professional finish. Whether icing cupcakes, edging a birthday cake or piping meringue atop lemon tarts, we use them all day long at Butter. We use piping bags to evenly and cleanly divide cupcake batter among the pans, glaze the top of cinny buns or write a birthday message on a cake. There is a wide choice of piping tips to choose from, but a large closed star tip, large and small round tips and a leaf tip are all you need to get started. If you plan to ice cookies, you may want to have several piping bags in your collection (or you can create disposable paper cornets from parchment paper, see page 140).

PAINTBRUSH

A tiny paintbrush comes in very handy when icing shaped cookies. It can help you move the icing around the cookie into tight spots without making a mess of it. A whole box can be found at your local dollar store for next to nothing.

Pastry

MARBLE

Marble countertops are a true luxury in any kitchen, as they can be very costly. A smaller piece of marble, about 24 × 24 inches, sitting on top of your existing counter, can be just as effective and is a much more affordable choice. Visit your local marble supplier to inquire about any end cuts they may have lying around and available for a deep discount. Your pastry will thank you, as the cool surface of the marble helps keep the butter in your pastry chilled while you roll it.

ROLLING PIN

A heavy rolling pin for rolling pastry, cookie and cinny bun dough is a must. One of the many things I inherited when I bought the old bakery space for Butter was a lovely collection of vintage wooden rolling pins that weigh a ton. They practically do the work for you. For home use I have a bright orange silicone rolling pin that does its job nicely and also serves as a threatening weapon should any thieves try to make off with my pies.

PASTRY BLENDER

A pastry blender or pastry cutter is a handy tool to have to cut butter into flour when making scones or pastry. It is a handheld tool with several wires or blades on one end which can be found at any kitchen supply store for as little as $5.

PASTRY DOCKER

This is a fantastic tool I started using only after I opened the bakery. Before that I used a fork to poke all the little holes in a pie shell before prebaking it, to let air escape. It worked just fine but took a little longer and didn't give as even and consistent a finish. At Butter we also run a pastry docker over graham cracker dough before cutting and baking it—it leaves the cracker with a lovely and familiar pattern.

PASTRY BRUSH

We use pastry brushes for lots of jobs in the kitchen at Butter, so I always make sure to have a couple floating around. I like the simple wooden ones with natural bristles. Watch closely when using one to coat the top of a pie or scone with egg wash as they sometimes lose a bristle or two.

Tools I Can't Live Without

DOUBLE BOILER

I think it is funny that this piece of equipment falls under the Tools I Can't Live Without—really, given how simple it is to recreate, I would say you *can* live without one! A flashy store-bought boiler is nice, but a simple heatproof bowl placed on top of a simmering pot of water on the stove will suffice every time—and take up less space in the cupboard. The purpose of the double boiler is to prevent the item you are heating or melting from burning. Always make sure that the simmering water does not touch the bottom of the bowl, or you may find yourself with this problem.

KITCHEN BLOWTORCH

This is one of the most fun tools to have in your kitchen. A little handheld blowtorch is perfect to easily brown meringue or toast the tops of the marshmallow on your Campfire Bar (page 106). In the old days, your mom browned the meringue on a lemon meringue pie in the oven, which offered little control. Now, with torch in hand, you have total creative control to brown as much or as little as you like. Kitchen blowtorches are available at most kitchen supply stores and, although they are costly at around $40, a good-quality one will last for years and years.

PARCHMENT PAPER

Another simple but necessary tool in the kitchen, parchment paper prevents cakes and cookies from sticking to the pan and makes cleanup a breeze. Don't be afraid to reuse parchment sheets as they will keep nicely for several rounds of baking. I also use parchment paper to sift dry ingredients onto (or you can use waxed paper, as a cheaper alternative). In a pinch, parchment paper can be folded to create a paper cornet for icing cookies and cakes (see page 140).

SCRAPERS

We use droves of scrapers at Butter. A metal bench scraper makes cleaning up the counters after rolling dough really quick and easy, and lends a hand when cutting or portioning dough. A plastic scraper ensures that the last bits of batter are scraped from the bowl; it also will remove any bits of dough left on the rolling pin.

SIFTER

I have an old hand-crank sifter at home, but time and time again I find it faster and easier to use a simple sieve and a piece of parchment paper. Just give the sieve a tap on the edge to sift the dry ingredients, and then use the parchment paper to transfer the dry ingredients to the mixer or mixing bowl.

SPATULAS

I have loads of spatulas and I don't believe there's a recipe in this book that doesn't require the use of one. I love the newer heat-resistant silicone spatulas because I no longer have to worry about melting them, like I did with the rubber ones! I particularly love my offset spatulas, both big and small. These are the secret to icing cakes, releasing butter tarts from the pan and spreading cinny bun filling across the dough. Who was the brilliant person who figured out that by simply putting a little bend in a metal spatula, every task would become infinitely easier?

STORAGE SUPPLIES

Nothing screams of a commercial kitchen more than containers labeled with a strip of masking tape and black-marker lettering identifying its contents. This works just as well at home, so save those yogurt and ice cream containers, as they make excellent vessels for storing toasted nuts, maple sauce and muffin batter. For storage options, grocery stores now offer an excellent selection of airtight containers in a variety of shapes and sizes, which have replaced the Tupperware of days of old. Affixing a strip of masking tape identifying the contents and the date they were stored saves you lots of time when hunting through the refrigerator or freezer.

THERMOMETERS

A candy thermometer and a chocolate thermometer will open a lot of creative doors for you in the kitchen. You will be making caramels, toffee and barks all day long—and need little more than some sugar or chocolate and a thermometer to do so. I love the accuracy and science behind them. No guessing involved, just patience and a watchful eye. The difference between the two thermometers is range of degrees. A basic candy thermometer has a range of from 100°F to 400°F and is marked with the various stages of candy making—hard ball, soft ball and so on. A chocolate thermometer does not read above 130°F and climbs in one-degree increments to ensure accurate tempering (see page 234).

TIMER

Anyone working in a commercial kitchen can tell you the importance of timers. We have them stashed all over the kitchen at Butter, as we usually have four bakers using the little kitchen at once. Things get hectic and bakers get distracted with other tasks, so the timer proves again and again to be one of their most important tools. An oven timer works well also, but a little portable one is best. It clips nicely to the top of your apron so you can go about your business without worry.

WOODEN SKEWERS

A container of wooden skewers is a must in the kitchen, and a large bag of them can be found at the dollar store or kitchen supply store. There is no quicker or more accurate way to determine if something is done than by inserting a wooden skewer into its center and checking for it to pull clean. We have a big canister of wooden skewers at the ready by the oven. One in each hand also works well to pierce the tops of cakes or loaves before glazing with syrup—the glaze runs into the holes and keeps the cake moist. 🅱

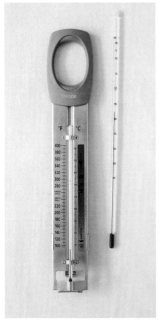

For successful baking, you'll need to know a few basic techniques. Success breeds confidence and confidence is a baker's secret weapon.

Successful Mixing and Whipping

CREAMING BUTTER AND SUGAR

An important part of baking most goodies is the creaming of the butter and sugar. It usually takes longer than you think it will, so you should plan to cream the butter and sugar for at least 5 minutes, maybe more. You want the two ingredients to go from yellow and grainy to pale, pale yellow and fluffy. If you are using brown sugar (rather than granulated), the mixture should become pale brown. Be sure to bring the butter to room temperature before you begin, as trying to cream cold butter will take a heck of a lot longer. The butter should be soft enough that your finger leaves an indentation when pressed in it, but not so soft that you can poke a finger right through it.

SCRAPING DOWN THE BOWL Most recipes in this book instruct you to scrape down the sides of the bowl several times when mixing to ensure that the butter, sugar, eggs and so on don't get left at the bottom of the mixing bowl. Not doing this is a huge rookie mistake at the bakery and one of the first lessons learned. A batter that has been properly blended will result in a consistent product. A batter that has *not* been properly blended will leave you with nasty sugar bubbles bursting on top or over the sides of your cupcakes or loaves.

FOLDING IN

Folding is a pretty simple technique that is used to incorporate the lighter part of a batter into the heavier part, while still trying to maintain as much air as possible—as with angel food cake (see page 166). You simply need to remember to cut, fold and turn. By this I mean cut the spatula down the center of the bowl of batter, scraping the bottom of the bowl as you go. Gently turn the batter over on itself to start to fold in the new ingredient. Turn the bowl slightly clockwise and repeat this process. Keep turning and repeating until everything is fully incorporated.

CUTTING IN

Cutting in is a way of incorporating butter or shortening into flour so that it leaves lumps (small pea-sized pieces) of the butter or shortening throughout the flour. This is important when making pastry because when the dough bakes, the butter lumps will heat up, melt and create steam, which gives you a nice flaky crust. The easiest way to cut in is using a pastry blender, but if you find yourself in a desperate pastry situation and you don't have one available, a pair of knives will work in a pinch. The technique is very straightforward. You simply use the blender to cut through the butter and flour mixture until you achieve the desired size of crumb. If you are using knives, place one in each hand and criss cross them through the dough like a pair of scissors.

WORKING WITH EGG WHITES

When separating egg whites from yolks, the rule of thumb is to avoid getting any yolk into the whites. If you do, you will have to start again from scratch, as any fat in the whites will prevent the whites from forming stiff peaks. For this reason you will also want to be sure to wipe the inside of the mixing bowl and whisk attachment very well before beginning to remove any traces of fat. If I am separating a lot of eggs for angel food cake or meringue, I crack each egg white into a small bowl, then transfer it to the larger mixing bowl. This way, should a yolk break in the process, I'll lose only one egg instead of the bowlful.

WHIPPING EGG WHITES
When whipping egg whites, you are looking for them to be glossy and smooth. Once you have achieved this, stop whipping, as it only takes a moment to pass this point and for the whites to look grainy and dull. A good test is to stick a spatula into the whipped egg whites, pull it out and turn it upright. You should have a firm and glossy peak of egg whites on the end of the spatula.

First Things First

BUTTER SIZE AND YIELDS

The baked goodies in this book are "Butter size." This may sound intimidating, as if Butter only creates treats for giants. Fear not! Butter's goodies are considered quite big, but there is something fun in the excess of it all.

If you want a smaller cookie, simply use a smaller scoop of dough. Even when I use regular-sized muffin pans, whether to make muffins or cupcakes, I like to fill them nearly full. This gives that nice round top I love. I know it's naughty, but I'm not really interested in eating the bottoms. Most of the cakes are made in standard 7-inch round cake pans and, depending on how big a slice you want, will yield about 8 to 10 slices. The same holds for the loaves, which will yield about 8 slices to 10 slices too. The yields for the cookie and cupcake recipes are approximate, as the numbers produced are directly related to how much cookie dough you nibble on or how much cupcake batter you lick from the spoon while you work. Not to worry, though, because everyone knows that anything you eat before it has baked has no calories! I can't remember where I heard this, but it works for me.

FREEZER IS NOT A BAD WORD

We couldn't run Butter without a freezer. There just wouldn't be enough time in the day or night to get everything done. A freezer is a godsend in the bakery world. So many kinds of dough, pastry shells, unbaked scones and even un-iced cakes can be frozen in advance, to be finished at a moment's notice. Remember this when you hesitate to make a full batch of cookies or pastry for fear you won't be able to eat it all. Sealed in plastic wrap, the dough will keep for at least 2 months in the freezer, and that can prove to be pretty handy when short on time. Always allow the dough you are using to completely defrost before working with it. Frozen dough can't be rolled, and frozen cookie dough is pretty hard to scoop and bake!

Before You Begin

READ THE RECIPE

Before beginning any baking, read the recipe through from start to finish. You want to ensure that you have all the ingredients on hand and a full understanding of the method. I can't stress enough the importance of being organized. I am all for being flexible and creative, but recipes are developed for a reason. Follow them step by step and success will be far more likely.

PREHEAT THE OVEN

The first thing to do after you have read through the recipe is set the oven to the required temperature. Preheating the oven is critical for successful baking. Too low a temperature will just melt the batter before it gets a chance to properly bake, making the end product tough; too high a temperature will bake the outside before the inside is done, resulting in a crusty exterior. It is also a good idea to routinely check the accuracy of your oven temperature using a secondary oven thermometer. If the oven's temperature setting does not match that of the secondary thermometer, adjust the oven accordingly. If the oven appears to be more than 20 degrees off, you should call your repairman and have him take a look.

I always opt for the center rack in the oven when baking. If you are baking several trays at once you may have to use the lower and upper racks also. If this is the case, then be sure to rotate the pans halfway through to ensure even baking.

PREPARE THE BAKING PANS

Greasing your baking pans is an important step in ensuring that the cake or loaf pops out in one piece. I use a small piece of waxed paper or parchment paper to help spread and evenly coat the inside of the pan with butter, making sure to get into the corners and up the sides. I then add about 1 tablespoon of all-purpose flour to the pan and gently tip it from side to side until the inside of the pan is evenly coated with a light dusting of flour. Remove any excess flour by giving the sides of the pan a light tap on the countertop and then tipping the excess out over the garbage bin.

When making bars, I like to grease the pan with butter and then line it with a piece of parchment paper large enough to extend past the edge of the pan on two sides. This creates two handles that are a great help when lifting the slab from the pan.

Never Forget

CLEAN AS YOU GO

I can't work at a messy desk, and I can't bake in a messy kitchen. It is so much easier to clean the few dirty dishes created as you work than it is to deal with a sink full of them when you're finished. Always have a clean damp cloth at the ready, and tuck a clean, dry cloth into the front of your apron or throw it over your shoulder. A big stack of clean cloths is imperative in any kitchen. We go through droves of them every day at Butter.

AND ONE MORE THING . . .

I often think that baked goods have a brain and must be outwitted. There is that moment when you are rolling pastry dough and you need to move it from the counter to the pie pan. A confident baker has no doubt when swiftly transporting the pastry; should you hesitate or question your ability for even a moment, the pastry wins. It cracks or tears and you find yourself cursing as you brace to start the process all over again. What you need to learn is the mantra I have used for years: *I will not be taken down by a piece of pastry.* I have muttered this mantra many times and in many iterations. Just insert the name of the baked good you are working on in lieu of the word *pastry*. It is important to show those cookies, cakes and all other baked goodies who the boss is! I promise: It works every time.

*D*on't be afraid to make mistakes, for even your mistakes will taste pretty good. There is no better way to learn than hands-on. Trust me when I tell you this: I am the lady who opened a bakery with literally no training, just some crazy optimism and a whole lot of confidence. I have made loads of mistakes along the way, but I have learned something each and every time. Like life, baking can be messy. We have good days and we have bad days. Sometimes your cake rises and sometimes it doesn't. Tomorrow is a fresh start. Tomorrow is another cake. *B*

Muffins, Scones, Cinny Buns and Loaves

Chapter 1

*E*very day at Butter we make a different muffin, with the exception of Wednesdays and Fridays. On those days we make Morning Glory Muffins. These muffins are so good, our customers demanded them twice a week. Well, actually, they asked nicely and we said okay.

Twice-a-Week (Morning Glory) Muffins

2 ½ cups all-purpose flour

1 ¾ cups granulated sugar

1 tablespoon cinnamon

2 teaspoons baking soda

2 cups grated carrots

1 cup sultana raisins

1 cup unsweetened shredded
    coconut

1 cup chopped pecans

1 large apple, peeled, cored and
    grated

4 large eggs

1 cup vegetable oil

1 tablespoon pure vanilla

MAKES: 12 muffins

YOU WILL NEED: muffin pan lined
    with paper liners, large ice
    cream scoop

1. Preheat the oven to 350°F.

2. In a large bowl, combine the flour, sugar, cinnamon, baking soda, carrots, raisins, coconut, pecans and apple and mix well.

3. In a separate bowl, whisk together the eggs, oil and vanilla.

4. Add the liquid ingredients to the dry ingredients and mix until just combined.

5. Use the ice cream scoop to divide the batter evenly between the paper liners.

6. Bake in the preheated oven for 35 minutes or until a wooden skewer inserted into the center comes out clean.

7. Remove from the oven and allow the muffins to cool slightly in the pan, then transfer to a wire rack to cool completely. (Or, if you just can't wait, split one while it is still warm and spread it with butter—yum!)

These muffins are just as good on the second day as they are on the first because of how moist the apple makes them. They also freeze really well, so make a large batch and tuck some away.

I'm not sure why, but I think if muffins were people, this one would be a true lady. Well-bred and dainty. Maybe she would wear a pretty hat. These muffins are lovely when made in miniature and served with tea.

Lemon Poppy Seed Muffins

¾ cup butter

3 cups all-purpose flour

1 tablespoon baking powder

½ teaspoon baking soda

½ teaspoon salt

1 ½ cups granulated sugar

¼ cup poppy seeds

1 cup sour cream

½ cup whole milk

½ cup lemon juice, freshly squeezed (about 2 lemons)

2 large eggs

Zest of 1 lemon

MAKES: 12 muffins (or 24 to 30 lady-like mini muffins)

YOU WILL NEED: muffin pan (or 2 mini muffin pans) buttered or lined with paper liners, large ice cream scoop (or small for mini muffins)

1. Preheat the oven to 350°F.

2. In a small saucepan over low heat, melt the butter (or melt in the microwave for about 30 seconds on high). Set aside to cool.

3. In a large bowl, combine the flour, baking powder, baking soda, salt, sugar and poppy seeds. Mix well to combine and to distribute the poppy seeds evenly.

4. In a separate bowl, whisk together the sour cream, milk, lemon juice, eggs and lemon zest. (The lemon juice may cause the milk to curdle, so do not be alarmed if it does.)

5. Add the liquid ingredients and melted butter to the dry ingredients and mix until just combined. Make sure to not overmix the batter.

6. Use the ice cream scoop to divide the batter evenly between the paper liners.

7. Bake in the preheated oven for 25 to 30 minutes or until a wooden skewer inserted into the center comes out clean.

8. Remove from the oven and allow the muffins to cool slightly in the pan, then transfer to a wire rack to cool completely.

I really like making these muffins little. I can't explain it, but I suspect it's so I can eat even more of them.

Little Pumpkin Pecan Muffins

24 whole pecans

½ cup plus 2 tablespoons butter

1 ¼ cups all-purpose flour

¾ teaspoon baking soda

1 ½ teaspoons cinnamon

¾ teaspoon ground ginger

½ teaspoon nutmeg

½ teaspoon ground cloves

½ teaspoon salt

1 cup pumpkin puree

2 large eggs

1 cup granulated sugar

¼ cup dark brown sugar

MAKES: **24 mini muffins**

YOU WILL NEED: **cookie sheet, 2 mini muffin pans buttered or lined with mini paper liners, small ice cream scoop**

For an alternative, but just as decadent an option, omit the pecans completely, and the butter, brown sugar and cinnamon in Step 6. Fold in 1 cup of dark chocolate chips after Step 5 instead, to make these Little Pumpkin Chocolate Chip Muffins!

1. Preheat the oven to 350°F.

2. Spread the pecans on a cookie sheet and toast them in the oven for 7 to 10 minutes, until nicely browned. Flip the nuts with a metal spatula at the halfway point to ensure even toasting. Remove from the oven and allow to cool.

3. In a small saucepan over low heat, melt ½ cup of the butter (or melt in the microwave for about 30 seconds on high). Set aside to cool.

4. Onto a large piece of parchment paper, sift together the flour, baking soda, 1 teaspoon of the cinnamon, the ground ginger, nutmeg, ground cloves and salt. Set aside.

5. In a large bowl, whisk together the melted butter, pumpkin, eggs and granulated sugar until well combined. Add the sifted dry ingredients and whisk until just combined.

6. In a small saucepan over a low heat, melt the remaining 2 tablespoons of butter (or melt in the microwave for about 30 seconds on high). Combine the butter with the brown sugar and the remaining ½ teaspoon of cinnamon.

7. Use the ice cream scoop to divide the batter evenly between the paper liners. Make sure not to fill them more than two-thirds full. Then use a teaspoon to make a small well in the center of each muffin and fill it with ½ teaspoon of the butter and brown sugar mixture. Top each muffin with a toasted pecan.

8. Bake in the preheated oven for 15 to 20 minutes or until the tops spring back when lightly pressed with your finger.

9 Remove from the oven and allow the muffins to cool slightly in the pan, then transfer to a wire rack to cool completely.

*S*omething happens when you sprinkle crumble topping on a muffin. It becomes a personal-sized cake just for one—no slicing or sharing required. To really personalize it, you can switch up the fruit in this recipe and use your own favorites. My husband likes them with peach—a lot!

Mixed Berry Crumble Top Muffins

¾ cup butter

3 cups all-purpose flour

1 ½ cups granulated sugar

1 tablespoon baking powder

½ teaspoon baking soda

½ teaspoon salt

2 cups mixed berries
 (blueberries, raspberries,
 blackberries or strawberries)

1 cup whole milk

1 cup sour cream

2 large eggs

CRUMBLE TOPPING

¾ cup all-purpose flour

¼ cup butter

¼ cup brown sugar

½ teaspoon cinnamon

⅛ teaspoon baking powder

Pinch of salt

MAKES: 12 muffins

YOU WILL NEED: muffin pan lined
 with paper liners, large ice
 cream scoop

1. Preheat the oven to 350°F.

2. In a small saucepan over low heat, melt the butter (or melt in the microwave for about 30 seconds on high). Set aside to cool.

3. In a large bowl, combine the flour, granulated sugar, baking powder, baking soda and salt. Mix well to combine. Add the berries and mix gently to coat the berries with the flour mixture.

4. In a separate bowl, whisk together the milk, sour cream and eggs.

5. Add the liquid ingredients and melted butter to the dry ingredients and mix until just combined. Be gentle with the berries (unless, of course, you want purple muffins!).

6. Prepare the crumble topping: In a bowl, combine the flour, butter, brown sugar, cinnamon, baking powder and salt. Mix with a fork until large, buttery crumbs form. Set aside.

7. Use the ice cream scoop to divide the batter evenly between the paper liners. Sprinkle the crumble topping over the top. You may have a little extra crumble topping left over, so don't feel you need to use it all.

8. Bake in the preheated oven for 25 to 30 minutes or until a wooden skewer inserted into the center comes out clean.

9. Remove from the oven and allow the muffins to cool slightly in the pan, then transfer to a wire rack to cool completely.

One of the best things about all of the muffins we make at Butter is that once you've measured out your ingredients, you don't require anything more than a mixing bowl and a large spoon to prepare them.

I think rhubarb needs to hire a PR firm to remind people how delicious it is. When it shows up at the farmers' market this summer, do your part to help its cause and buy some! Then go home and make these muffins and share them with your friends and family. Help get the word out. Rhubarb will thank you, and so will your taste buds.

Rhubarb Almond Muffins

¾ cup butter

3 cups all-purpose flour

1 ½ cups granulated sugar

1 tablespoon baking powder

½ teaspoon baking soda

½ teaspoon salt

2 cups rhubarb, chopped into 1-inch pieces

1 cup whole milk

1 cup sour cream

2 large eggs

1 tablespoon almond flavoring

1 cup sliced almonds

MAKES: **12 muffins**

YOU WILL NEED: **muffin pan lined with paper liners, large ice cream scoop**

1. Preheat the oven to 350°F.

2. In a small saucepan over low heat, melt the butter (or melt in the microwave for about 30 seconds on high). Set aside to cool.

3. In a large bowl, combine the flour, sugar, baking powder, baking soda and salt. Mix well to combine. Add the rhubarb and mix gently to coat the rhubarb with the flour mixture.

4. In a separate bowl, whisk together the milk, sour cream, eggs and almond flavoring.

5. Add the liquid ingredients and melted butter to the dry ingredients and mix until just combined.

6. Use the ice cream scoop to divide the batter evenly between the paper liners. Sprinkle the top of the batter with the sliced almonds.

7. Bake in the preheated oven for 25 to 30 minutes or until a wooden skewer inserted into the center comes out clean.

8. Remove from the oven and allow the muffins to cool slightly in the pan, then transfer to a wire rack to cool completely.

very day at Butter we make a different scone. There is no set schedule, so regular customers call us in the morning to check what we have on tap that day. This flavor never seems to disappoint, and when we tell them it's on the menu, they hightail it over to get one.

Pineapple Coconut Scones

5 cups all-purpose flour

1 ⅓ cups sugar

3 tablespoons baking powder

¼ teaspoon salt

1 ½ cups butter, chilled and cut into 1-inch cubes

2 cups unsweetened shredded coconut

¾ cup buttermilk

1 14-ounce can crushed pineapple with juice

FINISHING

1 large egg

2 tablespoons cold water

Coarse sanding sugar, for sprinkling

MAKES: 10 scones

YOU WILL NEED: cookie sheet, 3 ½-inch circular cutter

1. Preheat the oven to 400°F.

2. In a stand mixer fitted with a paddle attachment, quickly mix the flour, sugar, baking powder and salt on low speed to blend. Add the butter cubes and mix until large crumbs form. Add the coconut and mix again to distribute. Add the buttermilk, crushed pineapple and juice and mix until almost combined.

3. Turn the dough out onto a lightly floured work surface and roll out to about 1-inch thick (for tips on rolling dough see page 193). Use the circular cutter to cut out 10 circles and place them on the prepared cookie sheet about 1 ½ inches apart.

4. In a small bowl, whisk together the egg and water to make an egg wash. Use a pastry brush to gently coat the top of each scone with the wash. Sprinkle with a little sanding sugar.

5. Bake in the preheated oven for 20 to 25 minutes or until golden brown. A wooden skewer inserted into the center should come out clean.

6. Remove from the oven and allow the scones to cool on the cookie sheets. Then split them open and spread with lots of butter and jam!

I think if Canada were to have an official scone, this might just be it. Who should I contact about that? We need to make it happen! Please sign my Scone Petition at the back of this book.

Butterscotch Maple Pecan Scones

1 cup pecan pieces

5 cups all-purpose flour

1 ⅓ cups granulated sugar

3 tablespoons baking powder

¼ teaspoon salt

1 ½ cups butter, chilled and cut into
    1-inch cubes

2 cups butterscotch chips

1 ¾ cups buttermilk

¼ cup pure maple syrup

FINISHING

1 large egg

2 tablespoons cold water

Coarse sanding sugar, for sprinkling,
    or Maple Glaze (recipe follows)

MAPLE GLAZE

1 ¼ cups icing sugar

¼ cup pure maple syrup

½ teaspoon pure vanilla

½ cup maple flakes (optional)

MAKES: **10 scones**

YOU WILL NEED: **cookie sheet,
small piping bag fitted with
a round tip (optional),
3 ½-inch circular cutter**

1. Preheat the oven to 400°F.

2. Spread the pecans on the cookie sheet and toast in the oven for 7 to 10 minutes or until nicely browned. Flip the nuts with a metal spatula at the halfway point to ensure even toasting. Remove from the oven and allow to cool.

3. In a stand mixer fitted with a paddle attachment, quickly mix the flour, sugar, baking powder and salt on low speed to blend. Add the butter cubes and mix until large crumbs form. Add the butterscotch chips and pecan pieces and mix to incorporate.

4. Mix together the buttermilk and maple syrup. Add to the dry ingredients and mix until almost combined.

5. Turn the dough out onto a lightly floured work surface and roll out to about 1-inch thick (for tips on rolling dough see page 193). Use the circular cutter to cut out 10 circles and place them on the prepared cookie sheet about 1½ inches apart.

6. In a small bowl, whisk together the egg and water to make an egg wash. Use a pastry brush to gently coat the top of each scone with the wash. Sprinkle with a little sanding sugar. (If you plan to glaze the scones, skip the sugar sprinkle.)

7. Bake in the preheated oven for 20 to 25 minutes or until golden brown. A wooden skewer inserted into the center should come out clean.

8. Remove from the oven and allow the scones to cool before glazing.

9. Prepare the Maple Glaze: In a small bowl, whisk together the icing sugar, maple syrup and vanilla to create a thin glaze. Use the whisk to drizzle the glaze over the top of the cooled scones or fill the piping bag and pipe it over the top. If you have any maple flakes on hand, add a sprinkle on top of the maple glaze for an extra maple hit.

Maple flakes are a flaked version of maple sugar. They make a pretty finish on these scones and they further enhance their maple flavor. If you are lucky maple flakes will be found in your local grocery store near the maple syrup.

*T*his is one of the first scone flavors I came up with when I opened Butter. I had some apricots on hand, and the almond seemed like a natural fit. Then, out of the corner of my eye, I spied the white chocolate chips and all was right with the world.

Apricot White Chocolate Scones

5 cups all-purpose flour

1 ⅓ cups granulated sugar

3 tablespoons baking powder

¼ teaspoon salt

1 ½ cups butter, chilled and cut into
    1-inch cubes

2 cups dried apricots, chopped into
    ½-inch pieces

1 cup white chocolate chips

1 ¾ cups buttermilk

1 tablespoon almond flavoring

FINISHING

1 large egg

2 tablespoons cold water

Coarse sanding sugar, for sprinkling

MAKES: **10 scones**

YOU WILL NEED: **cookie sheet,
    3 ½-inch circular cutter**

1. Preheat the oven to 400°F.

2. In a stand mixer fitted with a paddle attachment, quickly mix the flour, sugar, baking powder and salt on low speed to blend. Add the butter cubes and mix until large crumbs form. Add the chopped apricots and white chocolate chips and mix again to incorporate.

3. Stir together the buttermilk and almond flavoring. Add to the dry ingredients and mix until almost combined.

4. Turn the dough out onto a lightly floured work surface and roll out to about 1-inch thick (for tips or rolling dough see page 193). Use the circular cutter to cut out 10 circles and place them on the prepared cookie sheet about 1 ½ inches apart.

5. In a small bowl, whisk together the egg and water to make an egg wash. Use a pastry brush to gently coat the top of each scone with the wash. Sprinkle with a little sanding sugar.

6. Bake in the preheated oven for 20 to 25 minutes or until golden brown. A wooden skewer inserted into the center should come out clean.

7. Remove from the oven and allow the scones to cool slightly. These scones are delicious served warm from the oven all on their own.

his scone is like breakfast in the palm of your hand. The only thing missing is some scrambled eggs on the side. I guess that is what your other hand is for.

Apple Bacon Cheddar Scones

8 slices bacon

5 cups all-purpose flour

⅓ cup granulated sugar

3 tablespoons baking powder

¼ teaspoon salt

1 ½ cups butter, chilled and cut into
   1-inch cubes

2 Granny Smith apples, peeled,
   cored and cut into ½-inch cubes

2 ½ cups grated sharp cheddar
   cheese

1 ¾ cups buttermilk

FINISHING

1 large egg

2 tablespoons cold water

MAKES: **10 scones**

YOU WILL NEED: **2 cookie sheets,
   3 ½-inch circular cutter**

These scones are best eaten
warm, straight out of the
oven, but they are almost
as delicious the next day
split open and toasted.

1. Preheat the oven to 400°F.

2. Place the bacon on the unlined cookie sheet and bake in the preheated oven for about 5 minutes. Remove from the oven, turn the bacon over and bake for another 5 to 7 minutes. Remove from the oven again and transfer the bacon to paper towel to cool. Pour the excess fat from the cookie sheet into a bowl and set aside (it should be about 2 tablespoons). When the bacon is cool, cut into ¹/₂-inch pieces.

3. In a stand mixer fitted with a paddle attachment, quickly mix the flour, sugar, baking powder and salt on low speed to blend. Add the butter cubes and mix until large crumbs form. Add the apple, bacon and 1 ¹/₂ cups of the cheddar cheese and mix to incorporate evenly.

4. Add the buttermilk to the reserved bacon fat and stir to blend. Add to the dry ingredients and mix until almost combined.

5. Turn the dough out onto a lightly floured work surface and roll out to about 1 inch thick (for tips on rolling dough see page 193). Use the circular cutter to cut out 10 circles and place them on the prepared cookie sheet about 1 ¹/₂ inches apart.

6. In a small bowl, whisk together the egg and water to make an egg wash. Use a pastry brush to gently coat the top of each scone with the wash. Sprinkle with the remaining 1 cup of cheddar cheese.

7. Bake in the preheated oven for 20 to 25 minutes or until golden brown. A wooden skewer inserted into the center should come out clean.

8. Remove from the oven and serve warm.

Saturday is a special day at Butter. We bake a lot of goodies that we don't have available during the week. It might be cruel, but we make our customers wait all week for our cinny buns. We make a different flavor every Saturday and I was feeling a little Southern on the day I came up with this one! You can change it up with different fruits and nuts to suit your taste. The bourbon glaze, however, will be a little hard to part with once you have tried it.

TODAY'S FLAVOR: Peach Pecan with Bourbon Glaze

Saturday Morning Cinny Buns

5 ½ cups all-purpose flour

1 tablespoon active dry yeast

1 ⅓ cups butter, room temperature

1 ¼ cups whole milk

⅓ cup granulated sugar

¾ teaspoon salt

3 large eggs

1 ½ cups dark brown sugar

2 tablespoons cinnamon

1 ½ cups pecans, lightly chopped

3 cups chopped peaches (3 to 4 peaches)

GLAZE

1 ¼ cups icing sugar

2 tablespoons heavy cream

1 ½ tablespoons bourbon

1 teaspoon clear corn syrup

½ teaspoon pure vanilla

MAKES: 12 cinny buns

YOU WILL NEED: (9- × 13-inch) baking pan buttered or lined with parchment paper, 2 cookie sheets

1. In a stand mixer fitted with a dough hook or paddle attachment, place 5 cups of the flour and the yeast and set aside.

2. In a large saucepan, combine ⅓ cup of the butter, the milk, granulated sugar and salt. Stir over medium heat until the milk is warm and the butter is melted.

3. Add the warm milk mixture to the yeast and flour and mix on low speed until incorporated. Add the eggs and continue to mix for about 6 to 7 minutes until the dough is shiny and smooth.

4. Lightly butter a large bowl and place the dough in it. Cover the bowl with a sheet of plastic wrap and place the bowl in a warm spot away from any drafts. Allow the dough to rise until it has doubled in size, about 90 minutes.

> Buttering the underside of the plastic wrap is a good idea to stop the dough sticking to it as it rises. I like to cover the bowl holding the rising dough with a clean tea towel to keep it warm.

5. Meanwhile, prepare the filling: In a stand mixer fitted with a paddle attachment, cream the remaining 1 cup of butter and the brown sugar on medium to high speed until light and fluffy.

6. Turn the mixer to low and add the remaining ½ cup of flour and the cinnamon and mix into a soft, spreadable paste.

7. Once the dough has fully risen, remove the plastic wrap and punch the dough down in the bowl to release the air produced by the yeast. Turn the dough out onto a lightly floured board and allow it to rest for about 10 minutes.

8. Spread the pecans on the cookie sheet and toast in the oven at 350°F for 7 to 10 minutes, until nicely browned. Flip the nuts with a metal spatula at the halfway point to ensure even toasting. Remove from the oven and allow to cool.

9. Transfer the dough to a lightly floured work surface and use a large rolling pin to roll it into a large rectangle, about 18 × 14 inches and about ¹/₂ inch thick (for tips on rolling dough see page 193).

10. Use a small offset spatula to spread the cinnamon paste evenly to the edges of the dough. Sprinkle the peach pieces and toasted pecans evenly on top of the cinnamon paste.

11. Carefully roll the dough up into a long log starting from the 18-inch side. Use a large, sharp knife to cut the dough into 12 equal rounds.

12. Place the rounds on the baking pan, sliced side up, and cover the pan with another piece of plastic wrap. Set in a warm place to rise until they have again doubled in size, about 90 minutes.

13. Preheat the oven to 350°F.

14. Bake in the preheated oven for 20 to 25 minutes or until the buns are a lovely golden brown and not sticky in the center. A wooden skewer inserted into the center should come out clean.

15. Remove from the oven and allow the buns to cool slightly, then turn them out of the pan onto a cookie sheet. Place a second cookie sheet on top of the buns and flip them over again. This brings the buns right side up on the sheet, ready for glazing.

16. Prepare the glaze: In a small bowl, whisk together the icing sugar, cream, bourbon, corn syrup and vanilla until the mixture becomes a nice runny glaze. Use the whisk to dribble the glaze over the top of the cinny buns—as much or as little as you like.

To save yourself time in the morning, prepare the dough the night before. Follow the recipe to Step 12 (covering the pan with plastic wrap) and then place the pan in the refrigerator overnight. Remove it in the morning in time to do the second rise of the dough (90 mins) and then continue with the recipe. This will give you extra-fresh, warm cinnamon buns, perfect for a special celebration (or just because it's Saturday).

*I*f there is one flavor that I feel represents Butter Baked Goods really well, it's pistachio. We love all things pistachio at the bakery. So, naturally, when I was trying to create an interesting pound cake, I turned to my favorite nut for assistance.

Chocolate Pistachio Pound Loaf

PISTACHIO BATTER

1 ⅔ cups all-purpose flour

½ teaspoon salt

1 cup butter, room temperature

1 cup granulated sugar

2 large eggs

1 tablespoon pure vanilla

2 tablespoons pistachio paste

CHOCOLATE BATTER

1 cup all-purpose flour

⅔ cup dark cocoa

½ teaspoon salt

1 cup butter, room temperature

1 cup granulated sugar

2 large eggs

1 tablespoon pure vanilla

MAKES: **2 loaves, 8 to 10 slices per loaf**

YOU WILL NEED: **2 (8-inch) loaf pans buttered and floured**

1. Preheat the oven to 350°F.

2. Prepare the pistachio batter: Onto a large piece of parchment paper, sift together the flour and salt. Set aside.

3. In a stand mixer fitted with a paddle attachment, cream the butter and sugar on medium to high speed until light and fluffy. Scrape down the sides of the bowl.

4. Add the eggs one at a time, and beat well after each addition. Scrape down the sides of the bowl. Add the vanilla and pistachio paste and beat to combine. Scrape down the sides of the bowl again.

5. Turn the mixer to low and slowly add the dry ingredients. Scrape down the sides of the bowl. Briefly mix again, then transfer the batter to another bowl.

6. Prepare the chocolate batter: Repeat Steps 2 to 5 with the chocolate batter ingredients, and sift the cocoa along with the flour and salt.

7. Divide the batters between the two loaf pans in a checkerboard pattern: To do this place one scoop of chocolate batter and one scoop of pistachio batter next to each other at one end of the loaf pan. Continue to fill the pan with rows of scoops of both batters, in alternate order to the batter in the row before. When the loaf pan is full, gently run a knife through the batter to create a swirl of the two flavors.

8. Bake in the preheated oven for 35 to 40 minutes or until a wooden skewer inserted into the center comes out clean.

9. Remove from the oven and allow to cool slightly, then transfer the loaves to wire racks to cool completely.

PISTACHIO . . . NOT JUST A PRETTY COLOR

If you don't have pistachio paste on hand, run out and get some! I believe it is one of those ingredients that you should never be without. If you can't find it at your local grocery store, please persevere. Even if you find yourself cursing me while you drive to some distant gourmet shop, I promise you will thank me in the end. And for an added bonus, sprinkle ¼ cup chopped pistachios on top of the batter before you put the loaf pans in the oven.

I have yet to meet someone who doesn't like banana bread. If you are out there, call me, because we need to talk. This recipe makes enough for two large loaves—one for you and one for me.

Banana Chocolate Loaf

3 ½ cups all-purpose flour

2 teaspoons baking soda

1 teaspoon salt

1 cup butter, room temperature

1 ¾ cups granulated sugar

4 large eggs

3 large bananas, mashed

1 cup sour cream

1 tablespoon pure vanilla

1 ¼ cups dark chocolate chips

MAKES: 2 loaves, about 8 to 10 slices per loaf

YOU WILL NEED: 2 (8-inch) loaf pans buttered and floured

1. Preheat the oven to 350°F.

2. Onto a large piece of parchment paper, sift together the flour, baking soda and salt. Set aside.

3. In a stand mixer fitted with a paddle attachment, cream the butter and sugar on medium to high speed until light and fluffy. Scrape down the sides of the bowl.

4. Add the eggs one at a time, and beat well after each addition. Scrape down the sides of the bowl again. Add the mashed bananas, sour cream and vanilla and mix to combine.

5. Turn the mixer to low and slowly add the dry ingredients and mix until just combined. Add the chocolate chips and mix to distribute evenly.

6. Pour the batter evenly between the two prepared pans. Use a spatula to spread the batter smoothly across the pans.

7. Bake in the preheated oven for 45 to 50 minutes or until a wooden skewer inserted into the center comes out clean.

8. Remove from the oven and allow the loaves to cool slightly, then transfer to a wire rack to cool completely. Use a serrated knife to slice the loaves, then serve.

This is the first recipe that I asked my mother-in-law to share with me. Mary Daykin is a great woman, an enthusiastic baker and, at 91, still winning gold at the Seniors Games for the 10K walk. A slice of this loaf is great alongside a cup of tea, or you can take it up a notch and ice it with Cream Cheese Butter Cream (page 135).

Grandma Daykin's Zucchini Loaf

3 cups all-purpose flour

1 tablespoon cinnamon

1 teaspoon pumpkin pie spice

1 teaspoon salt

1 teaspoon baking soda

¼ teaspoon baking powder

2 large eggs

2 cups grated raw zucchini

1 ½ cups sugar

1 cup vegetable oil

1 tablespoon pure vanilla

MAKES: 2 loaves, about 8 to 10 slices per loaf

YOU WILL NEED: 2 (8-inch) loaf pans buttered and floured

1. Preheat the oven to 325°F.

2. Onto a large piece of parchment paper, sift together the flour, cinnamon, pumpkin pie spice, salt, baking soda and baking powder. Set aside.

3. In a stand mixer fitted with the paddle attachment, beat the eggs on medium speed until light and fluffy. Add the zucchini, sugar, oil and vanilla and mix to blend.

4. Turn the mixer to low and slowly add the dry ingredients and mix until just blended. Scrape down the sides of the bowl.

5. Pour the batter evenly between the two prepared pans. Use a spatula to spread the batter smoothly across the pans.

6. Bake in the preheated oven for about 60 minutes or until a wooden skewer inserted into the center comes out clean.

7. Remove from the oven and allow the loaves to cool slightly, then transfer to a wire rack to cool completely. Use a serrated knife to slice the loaves, then serve.

Drop and Sandwich Cookies

Chapter 2

*P*eanut butter cookies are fantastic, no argument there. But two peanut butter cookies—with a generous helping of peanut butter filling sandwiched between them—is simply out of this world.

The Peanut Butter Sandwich Cookie

COOKIES

2 ¼ cups all-purpose flour

½ teaspoon baking soda

½ teaspoon salt

1 cup butter, room temperature

1 cup smooth peanut butter

¾ cup granulated sugar

¾ cup dark brown sugar

1 large egg

1 teaspoon pure vanilla

FILLING

1 cup smooth peanut butter

½ cup butter, room temperature

2 cups icing sugar

½ cup heavy cream

MAKES: 12 sandwich cookies

YOU WILL NEED: 2 cookie sheets lined with parchment paper, medium ice cream scoop

1. Preheat the oven to 350°F.

2. Onto a large piece of parchment paper, sift together the flour, baking soda and salt. Set aside.

3. In a stand mixer fitted with a paddle attachment, cream the butter and peanut butter on medium to high speed until well blended. Add the granulated and dark brown sugars and continue to cream until light and fluffy.

4. Add the egg and beat briefly. Scrape down the sides of the bowl. Add the vanilla and beat again to combine. Scrape down the sides of the bowl again.

5. Turn the mixer to low and add the dry ingredients and mix until fully combined.

6. Use the ice cream scoop to drop 24 equally sized portions of dough onto the prepared cookie sheets, about 1 ½ inches apart. Hold your three middle fingers together and press down on the top of each to make slight indentations across the top.

7. Bake in the preheated oven for 15 to 17 minutes or until the cookies are lightly golden brown around the edges. Take care not to overbake the cookies as crunchy sandwiches can be hard to eat!

8. Remove from the oven and transfer the cookies to wire racks to cool completely.

9. Meanwhile, prepare the filling: In a stand mixer fitted with a paddle attachment, cream the peanut butter and butter on medium to high speed until light and fluffy. Add the icing sugar and continue to cream until well combined.

10. Turn the mixer to low and slowly add the cream. Gradually increase the speed of the mixer and continue to beat until the mixture is smooth and creamy.

11. When the cookies have cooled, turn 12 of them bottom side up. Spoon 2 heaping tablespoons of filling onto each. Place the remaining cookies on top and press down lightly until the butter cream has spread to the edges of the cookies. You have just created the perfect cookie sandwich!

his cookie is far and away our best seller. The same week that O, the Oprah magazine, was considering them for its Christmas list, Vancouver Magazine named them one of the 101 Things to Taste Before You Die. Literally overnight we had to hire someone to just make this cookie all day long! I can't believe I am sharing this recipe. Am I nuts?

The Homemade You-Know-What

COOKIES

3 cups all-purpose flour

¾ cup dark cocoa

1 teaspoon baking soda

½ teaspoon salt

¼ teaspoon baking powder

1 ½ cups butter, room temperature

2 cups granulated sugar, plus extra
   for the cookie tops

2 large eggs

1 teaspoon pure vanilla

FILLING

1 cup butter, room temperature

2 cups icing sugar

1 tablespoon pure vanilla

MAKES: **12 sandwich cookies**

YOU WILL NEED: **2 cookie sheets
   lined with parchment paper,
   medium ice cream scoop**

1. Preheat the oven to 350°F.

2. Onto a large piece of parchment paper, sift together the flour, cocoa, baking soda, salt and baking powder. Set aside.

3. In a stand mixer fitted with a paddle attachment, cream the butter and sugar on medium to high speed until light and fluffy. Scrape down the sides of the bowl.

4. Add the eggs one at a time and beat briefly after each addition. Scrape down the sides of the bowl. Add the vanilla and beat again to combine. Scrape down the sides of the bowl again.

5. Turn the mixer to low and add the dry ingredients and mix until fully combined.

6. Use the ice cream scoop to drop 24 equally sized portions of dough onto the prepared cookie sheets, about 1 ¹/₂ inches apart. Fill a small bowl with granulated sugar. Press a drinking glass or flat-bottomed mug onto a dough portion to make the bottom of the glass a little sticky with dough. Dip the glass into the bowl of sugar to coat and then press down slightly onto the dough again to transfer the sugar. Repeat for each cookie until they are all topped with sugar.

7. Bake in the preheated oven for 15 to 17 minutes or until the cookies are firm around the edges but still slightly soft in the center.

8. Remove from the oven and transfer the cookies to wire racks to cool completely.

9. Meanwhile, prepare the filling: In a stand mixer fitted with a paddle attachment, cream the butter and icing sugar on medium to high speed until pale in color. Add the vanilla, increase the speed to high and continue to cream until the filling is light and fluffy.

10. When the cookies have cooled, turn 12 of them bottom side up. Spoon 2 heaping tablespoons of filling onto each. Place the remaining cookies on top and press down lightly until the butter cream has spread to the edges of the cookies. Stack them high on a cake plate and holler for your friends and family.

*I*n 2010, the Winter Olympics came to Vancouver. It was an exciting time and really brought the city together. To celebrate this momentous occasion, we created a few new treats with a distinctly Canadian vibe. This cookie was one of them. The intention was just to have them around while the world was watching, but they proved so popular, we are still making them.

Maple Snickerdoodle Sandwich Cookies

COOKIES

2 ½ cups all-purpose flour

2 teaspoons cream of tartar

1 teaspoon baking soda

½ teaspoon salt

¾ cup butter, room temperature

1 ¼ cups granulated sugar

2 large eggs

½ teaspoon pure vanilla

FINISHING

¼ cup granulated sugar

2 tablespoons cinnamon

FILLING

1 cup butter, room temperature

2 cups icing sugar

½ cup pure maple syrup

MAKES: 12 sandwich cookies or 24 single cookies

YOU WILL NEED: 2 cookie sheets lined with parchment paper, medium ice cream scoop

1. Preheat the oven to 350°F.

2. Onto a large piece of parchment paper, sift together the flour, cream of tartar, baking soda and salt. Set aside.

3. In a stand mixer fitted with a paddle attachment, cream the butter and sugar on medium to high speed until light and fluffy. Scrape down the sides of the bowl.

4. Add the eggs one at a time and beat briefly after each addition. Scrape down the sides of the bowl. Add the vanilla and beat again to combine. Scrape down the sides of the bowl again.

5. Turn the mixer to low and add the dry ingredients and mix until fully combined.

6. In a small bowl, combine the granulated sugar and cinnamon. Use the ice cream scoop to drop 24 equally sized portions of dough, one at a time, into the cinnamon sugar. Use your fingers to roll the dough around to coat on all sides, then place on the prepared cookie sheets about 1 1/2 inches apart. Use the palm of your hand to press down lightly on the top of each portion to flatten slightly.

7. Bake in the preheated oven for 15 to 17 minutes or until the cookies are firm around the edges but still slightly soft in the center.

8. Remove from the oven and transfer the cookies to a wire rack to cool completely.

9. Meanwhile, prepare the filling: In a stand mixer fitted with a paddle attachment, cream the butter and icing sugar on medium to high speed until very pale in color. Add the maple syrup, increase the speed to high and continue mixing until the filling is light and fluffy.

10. When the cookies have cooled, turn 12 of them bottom side up. Spoon 2 heaping tablespoons of filling onto each. Place the remaining cookies on top and press down lightly until the butter cream has spread to the edges of the cookies.

You can skip the butter cream filling if you are in a rush, because this cookie is just as good on its own.

*S*ometimes the simplest things in life are the most satisfying. There are no bits and bobs in this cookie. Just a lovely crunch as your teeth sink through to the chewy goodness.

Big Sugar Cookies

4 cups all-purpose flour

1 ½ teaspoons baking soda

½ teaspoon salt

¾ cup butter, room temperature

¾ cup vegetable oil

2 cups granulated sugar

2 large eggs

1 teaspoon pure vanilla

Coarse sanding sugar, for sprinkling

MAKES: **24 cookies**

YOU WILL NEED: **2 cookie sheets lined with parchment paper, medium ice cream scoop**

1. Preheat the oven to 350°F.

2. Onto a large piece of parchment paper, sift together the flour, baking soda and salt. Set aside.

3. In a stand mixer fitted with a paddle attachment, cream the butter and oil on medium to high heat until light and fluffy, about 3 minutes. Scrape down the sides of the bowl.

4. Add the sugar and mix until well combined. Scrape down the sides of the bowl. Add the eggs one at a time and beat briefly after each addition. Add the vanilla and beat again to combine. Scrape down the sides of the bowl.

5. Turn the mixer to low and add the dry ingredients and mix until fully combined. The dough should be quite pale in color.

6. Use the ice cream scoop to drop 24 equally sized portions of dough onto the prepared cookie sheets, about 1 ½ inches apart. Use the palm of your hand to press down lightly on the top of each dough portion to flatten slightly, then sprinkle with a little sanding sugar.

7. Bake in the preheated oven for 15 to 17 minutes or until the cookies are lightly golden around the edges and cracked in the center.

8. Remove from the oven and transfer the cookies to wire racks to cool.

*W*hen I first opened the bakery this cookie just had raisins in it. But then one day I got to thinking that it needed a little something extra to set it apart from all the other oatmeal cookies out there. A makeover was in order. It's amazing what a new haircut and a little lipstick can do!

Oatmeal Cranberry Pecan Cookies
(With a little white chocolate, too!)

2 cups all-purpose flour

1 teaspoon baking powder

1 teaspoon baking soda

½ teaspoon salt

⅔ cup pecans, lightly chopped

1 cup butter, room temperature

1 ¼ cups dark brown sugar

¾ cup granulated sugar

2 large eggs

1 teaspoon pure vanilla

1 ½ cups large-flake rolled oats

⅔ cup white chocolate chips

⅔ cup dried cranberries

MAKES: **24 cookies**

YOU WILL NEED: **2 cookie sheets lined with parchment paper, medium ice cream scoop**

1. Preheat the oven to 350°F.

2. Onto a large piece of parchment paper, sift together the flour, baking powder, baking soda and salt. Set aside.

3. Place the pecans on the cookie sheet and bake in the preheated oven for about 10 minutes or until lightly toasted. Flip the nuts with a metal spatula at the halfway point to ensure even toasting. Remove from the oven and set aside to cool.

4. In a stand mixer fitted with a paddle attachment, cream the butter and both sugars on medium to high speed until light and fluffy. Scrape down the sides of the bowl.

5. Add the eggs one at a time and beat briefly after each addition. Scrape down the sides of the bowl. Add the vanilla and beat again to combine. Scrape down the sides of the bowl.

6. Turn the mixer to low and add the dry ingredients and the oats and mix until combined. Add the white chocolate chips, pecans and cranberries and mix again to fully distribute.

7. Use the ice cream scoop to drop 24 equally sized portions of dough onto the prepared cookie sheets, about 1 ¹/₂ inches apart. Use the palm of your hand to press down lightly on the top of each cookie to flatten slightly.

8. Bake in the preheated oven for 15 to 17 minutes or until lightly golden around the edges and slightly soft in the center.

9. Remove from the oven and transfer to wire racks to cool completely.

*I*f Butter Baked Goods were on fire, this would be the cookie my husband, Paul, would run in to save. He is not alone, as it proves to be a favorite with a lot of people, myself included. The secret to making these cookies taste so good lies in toasting the nuts and using the best dark chocolate chips you can find.

The Nutty Chocolate Chip Cookie

2 ½ cups all-purpose flour

1 teaspoon baking soda

½ teaspoon salt

1 ¼ cups walnuts

1 ¼ cups pecans

1 cup butter, room temperature

1 ¼ cups dark brown sugar

¾ cup granulated sugar

2 large eggs

2 cups dark chocolate chips

MAKES: **30 cookies**

YOU WILL NEED: **2 cookie sheets lined with parchment paper, medium ice cream scoop**

1. Preheat the oven to 350°F.

2. Onto a large piece of parchment paper, sift together the flour, baking soda and salt. Set aside.

3. Place the walnuts and pecans on the cookie sheet and bake in the preheated oven for about 10 minutes or until lightly toasted. Flip the nuts with a metal spatula at the halfway point to ensure even toasting. Remove from the oven and set aside to cool.

4. In a stand mixer fitted with a paddle attachment, cream the butter and both sugars on medium to high speed until light and fluffy.

5. Add the eggs one at a time and beat after each addition. Scrape down the sides of the bowl and beat again for a moment.

6. Turn the mixer to low and add the dry ingredients and mix until fully combined. Add the chocolate chips and cooled nuts and mix to fully distribute.

7. Use the ice cream scoop to drop 30 equally sized portions of dough onto the prepared cookie sheets, about 1 ½ inches apart.

8. Bake in the preheated oven for 12 to 15 minutes or until the cookies are lightly browned around the edges and still slightly soft in the center.

9. Remove from the oven and transfer to wire racks to cool. The cookies will firm up as they cool but will remain chewy.

This recipe makes a pretty good-sized batch of cookies so you can always scoop and freeze some of the dough balls instead of baking them all at once. That way you'll have them ready to bake the next time you crave a warm cookie straight from the oven.

*T*his is one for chocolate lovers. Deep and dark, with a soft chewy center—plus the addition of a little bit of espresso gives this cookie a nice kick. Given the combo of chocolate and espresso, this may not be the best cookie to snack on right before bed, but it could be a heck of a way to start your day!

Chocolate Espresso White Chocolate Cookies

2 cups all-purpose flour

½ cup dark cocoa

2 tablespoons instant espresso powder

1 teaspoon baking soda

1 teaspoon salt

1 cup butter, room temperature

¾ cup granulated sugar

¾ cup dark brown sugar

2 large eggs

1 ½ teaspoons pure vanilla

1 ½ cups white chocolate chips

1 cup dark chocolate chips

MAKES: **24 cookies**

YOU WILL NEED: **2 cookie sheets lined with parchment paper, medium ice cream scoop**

1. Preheat the oven to 350°F.

2. Onto a large piece of parchment paper, sift together the flour, cocoa, espresso powder, baking soda and salt. Set aside.

3. In a stand mixer fitted with a paddle attachment, cream the butter and both sugars on medium to high speed until light and fluffy. Scrape down the sides of the bowl.

4. Add the eggs one at a time and beat briefly after each addition. Scrape down the sides of the bowl. Add the vanilla and beat again to combine. Scrape down the sides of the bowl.

5. Turn the mixer to low and add the dry ingredients and mix until fully combined. Add the white and dark chocolate chips and mix again to fully distribute.

6. Use the ice cream scoop to drop 24 equally sized portions of dough onto the prepared cookie sheets, about 1 ½ inches apart. Use the palm of your hand to press down lightly on the top of each to flatten slightly.

7. Bake in the preheated oven for 15 to 17 minutes or until the cookies are firm around the edges but still slightly soft in the center.

8. Remove from the oven and transfer the cookies to wire racks to cool.

*M*y daughter, India, named this cookie when she was two years old (she also coined the terms bed-nite snack and real-live action movie, but that's another story . . .). Soft and chewy, there is no snap to be found in this ginger cookie.

The Gingerstamp

4 cups all-purpose flour

2 ½ teaspoons baking soda

2 teaspoons ground ginger

1 teaspoon cinnamon

½ teaspoon ground cloves

½ teaspoon salt

¾ cup butter, room temperature

2 ½ cups granulated sugar

3 large eggs

½ cup fancy molasses

1 teaspoon pure vanilla

MAKES: 24 cookies

YOU WILL NEED: 2 cookie sheets lined with parchment paper, medium ice cream scoop

1. Preheat the oven to 350°F.

2. Onto a large piece of parchment paper, sift together the flour, baking soda, ground ginger, cinnamon, ground cloves and salt. Set aside.

3. In a stand mixer fitted with a paddle attachment, cream the butter and 2 cups of the sugar on medium to high speed until light and fluffy. Scrape down the sides of the bowl.

4. Add the eggs one at a time and beat briefly after each addition. Scrape down the sides of the bowl. Add the molasses and vanilla. Continue to mix on high until the molasses and vanilla are well combined and the mixture is pale in color. Scrape down the sides of the bowl.

5. Turn the mixer to low and add the dry ingredients and mix until fully combined.

6. In a small bowl add the remaining ½ cup of sugar. Use the ice cream scoop to drop 24 equally sized portions of dough, one at a time, into the sugar. Use your fingers to roll the dough around to coat on all sides, then place the cookies on the prepared cookie sheets about 1½ inches apart. Use the palm of your hand to press down lightly on the top of each portion to flatten slightly.

7. Bake in the preheated oven for 15 to 17 minutes or until the cookies are firm around the edges but still slightly soft in the center.

8. Remove from the oven and transfer the cookies to wire racks to cool.

I love the salty-sweet combination of this cookie—it is pure magic. And it's also a little like my husband and me. Mostly sweet, but every now and then one of us can be a little salty.

Sticks and Stones Cookies

2 ½ cups all-purpose flour

1 teaspoon baking soda

½ teaspoon salt

¾ cup butter, room temperature

¾ cup granulated sugar

¾ cup brown sugar

2 large eggs

1 teaspoon pure vanilla

2 large bags of Smarties or M&M's (some for the cookies, and some for you)

1 bag of pretzel sticks (about 120 sticks), broken in half

MAKES: **24 cookies**

YOU WILL NEED: **2 cookie sheets lined with parchment paper, medium ice cream scoop**

1. Preheat the oven to 350°F.

2. Onto a large piece of parchment paper, sift together the flour, baking soda and salt. Set aside.

3. In a stand mixer fitted with a paddle attachment, cream the butter and both sugars on medium to high speed until light and fluffy. Scrape down the sides of the bowl.

4. Add the eggs one at time and beat briefly after each addition. Scrape down the sides of the bowl. Add the vanilla and beat again to combine. Scrape down the sides of the bowl.

5. Turn the mixer to low and add the dry ingredients and mix until fully combined.

6. Use the ice cream scoop to drop 24 equally sized portions of dough onto the prepared cookie sheets, about 1 $^1/_2$ inches apart. The cookies will spread as they bake, so there is no need to flatten them.

7. Divide the Smarties or M&M's between the portions of dough and press into the top of each. Then poke about 10 pretzel stick halves into the top and sides.

8. Bake in the preheated oven for 15 to 17 minutes or until the cookies are golden brown around the edges but still soft in the center.

9. Remove from the oven and transfer the cookies to wire racks to cool.

Rolled and Cut

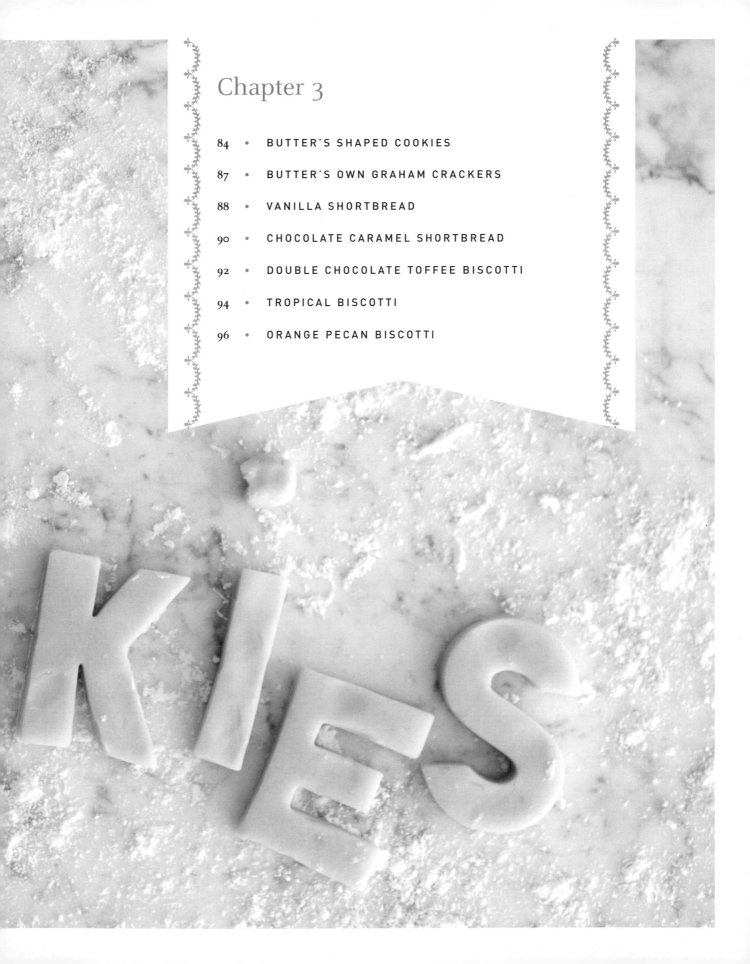

Chapter 3

*S*ome of the most fun we have at the bakery involves coming up with different shaped cookies, depending on the season, the holiday and our mood. Remember that a cookie cutter is only a shape so you are limited only by your imagination! Cookies shaped like bouquets of flowers easily become heads of broccoli, and fish-shaped cookies can happily become carrots.

Butter's Shaped Cookies

3 cups all-purpose flour

1 ½ teaspoons baking powder

1 ½ cups butter, room temperature

¾ cup icing sugar

½ cup granulated sugar

2 tablespoons pure vanilla

ICING
Royal Icing (page 136)

Variety of food colorings (as desired)

MAKES: About 24 cookies (using a 3 ½-inch cutter)

YOU WILL NEED: 2 cookie sheets lined with parchment paper, cookie cutters of your choice

1. Preheat the oven to 350°F.

2. Onto a large piece of parchment paper, sift together the flour and baking powder. Set aside.

3. In a stand mixer fitted with a paddle attachment, cream the butter and sugars on medium to high speed until light and fluffy. Scrape down the sides of the bowl. Add the vanilla and mix to combine. Scrape down the sides of the bowl again.

4. Turn the mixer to low and add the dry ingredients and mix until fully combined.

5. Shape the dough into a large disk about 1 inch thick and wrap in plastic wrap. Chill in the refrigerator for at least 1 hour.

6. Divide the disk into two, and place half the dough on a lightly floured work surface. Use a rolling pin to roll out the dough to about ¼ inch thick.

ROLLING COOKIE DOUGH
A good technique for rolling cookie dough, to ensure even thickness, is to use two yard sticks (about ¼ inch thick each). Place the yard sticks on the work surface on either side of your unrolled cookie dough. Roll the dough until it reaches the same thickness as the yard sticks and the rolling pin is resting on top of them.

7. Use the cookie cutter of your choice to cut out about 12 cookies. Carefully transfer to the prepared cookie sheets and place about ¹/₂ inch apart. You may have to combine the dough scraps and reroll the dough to cut out enough cookies. Avoid doing this too many times, as the cookies will become tough with overhandling.

8. Use a rolling pin to roll out the second disk of dough to about ¹/₄ inch thick and repeat Step 7.

9. Bake in the preheated oven for 15 minutes or until the cookies are lightly browned around the edges.

10. Remove from the oven and allow the cookies to cool for about 10 minutes on the sheets, then transfer to wire racks to cool completely.

You'll find my tips on Icing Cookies on page 142. If you are in a rush or don't feel like letting your little ones make a mess with Royal Icing, you can sprinkle these cookies with various colors of sanding sugars prior to baking. This gives a really fun effect.

I came up with this recipe the day I decided to create a homemade s'more (see page 237) and needed to create a cracker worthy of our fabulous marshmallows. Goal achieved! Then I discovered that these graham crackers are so good, they're just as delicious all on their own. So there, Mr. Perfect Marshmallow, take that!

Butter's Own Graham Crackers

2 cups all-purpose flour

2 cups graham crumbs

2 teaspoons baking soda

2 teaspoons cinnamon

1 teaspoon salt

1 ⅓ cups butter, room temperature

1 cup light brown sugar

1 cup liquid honey

MAKES: About 24 s'more crackers or 12 thicker cookies

YOU WILL NEED: 2 cookie sheets lined with parchment paper, pastry docker

1. Preheat the oven to 350°F.

2. Onto a large piece of parchment paper, sift together the flour, graham crumbs, baking soda, cinnamon and salt. Set aside.

3. In a stand mixer fitted with a paddle attachment, cream the butter, sugar and honey on medium to high speed until light and fluffy. Scrape down the sides of the bowl.

4. Turn the mixer to low and add the dry ingredients and mix until fully combined.

5. Place the dough on a lightly floured work surface. Use a rolling pin to roll out the dough to about ¼ inch thick for s'more crackers and ½ inch thick for cookies (for tips on rolling cookie dough see page 84). Roll the pastry docker over the dough to create a dotted pattern.

6. Use a paring knife to cut the dough into 2-inch squares. Use an offset spatula to carefully transfer to the prepared cookie sheets and place about 1 inch apart.

6. Bake in the preheated oven for 8 to 10 minutes or until the crackers are lightly golden all over. The thicker cookie versions may need an extra couple of minutes.

7. Remove from the oven and transfer the crackers or cookies to wire racks to cool.

I used to believe that shortbread was only for the Christmas season. My customers convinced me otherwise, and they were right! We sell these cookies in bags of six at Butter, because one would never be enough.

Vanilla Shortbread

1 cup butter, room temperature

1 cup icing sugar

2 ¼ cups all-purpose flour

2 tablespoons pure vanilla

FINISHING
½ cup granulated sugar, for
    dusting

MAKES: About 24 cookies

YOU WILL NEED: 2 cookie sheets
    lined with parchment paper,
    2 ½-inch circular cutter with
    scalloped edge

1. Preheat the oven to 325°F.

2. In a stand mixer fitted with a paddle attachment, cream the butter and icing sugar on medium to high speed until light and fluffy. Scrape down the sides of the bowl.

3. Turn the mixer to low and add the flour and mix until just combined. Scrape down the sides of the bowl. Add the vanilla and mix to combine.

4. Place the dough on a lightly floured work surface. Use a rolling pin to roll out the dough to about ¹/₄ inch thick (for tips on rolling cookie dough see page 84). Use the circular cutter to cut out 24 circles. Carefully transfer to the prepared cookie sheets and place about ¹/₂ inch apart.

5. Bake in the preheated oven for 15 minutes or until the cookies are lightly golden brown around the edges.

6. Remove from the oven and sprinkle the cookies generously with granulated sugar while still warm. Transfer to wire racks to cool.

Adding the zest of 1 lemon and 1 tablespoon of Earl Grey tea leaves to this recipe makes a lovely variation. Add them after creaming the butter and sugar, but before you add the flour.

hocolate shortbread is a lovely treat just as it is, but I can never leave well enough alone. I got to thinking, if chocolate is good and caramel is good, then together they should be doubly so.

Chocolate Caramel Shortbread

2 cups all-purpose flour

½ cup dark cocoa

½ teaspoon salt

1 cup butter, room temperature

½ cup icing sugar

1 teaspoon pure vanilla

1 jar dulce de leche (you won't need the whole jar, but I know you will find lots of yummy ways to use up any leftovers!)

FINISHING

1 cup dark chocolate chips

2 tablespoons butter

MAKES: 12 sandwich cookies or about 24 single cookies

YOU WILL NEED: 2 cookie sheets lined with parchment paper, 2 ¾-inch cookie cutter

1. Preheat the oven to 350°F.

2. Onto a large piece of parchment paper, sift together the flour, cocoa and salt. Set aside.

3. In a stand mixer fitted with a paddle attachment, cream the butter and icing sugar on medium to high speed until light and fluffy. Scrape down the sides of the bowl. Add the vanilla and mix to combine. Scrape down the sides of the bowl again.

4. Turn the mixer to low and add the dry ingredients and mix until fully combined.

5. Shape the dough into a large disk and wrap in plastic wrap. Chill in the refrigerator for 30 minutes.

6. Divide the disk into two, and place half the dough on a lightly floured work surface. Use a rolling pin to roll out the dough to about ¼ inch thick (for tips on rolling cookie dough see page 84). Use the cookie cutter of your choice to cut out 12 cookies. Carefully transfer to the prepared cookie sheets and place about ½ inch apart.

7. Repeat Step 6 with the remaining half of the dough.

8. Bake in the preheated oven for 15 to 17 minutes or until firm around the edges.

9. Remove from the oven and allow the cookies to cool briefly on the sheets, then transfer to wire racks to cool completely.

10. Turn 12 of the cookies bottom side up and spoon 1 teaspoon of dulce de leche onto each. Place the remaining cookies on top to create little sandwiches.

11. To finish: In a double boiler, or in a heatproof bowl set over a saucepan of simmering water, melt together the chocolate chips and butter. Dip one half of each cookie sandwich into the chocolate until it reaches the center line of the cookie. Place on a piece of parchment paper until the chocolate has set.

For Valentine's Day we use a heart-shaped cookie cutter for these cookies, but for the rest of the year a circular cutter with a scalloped edge makes them look just as lovely.

I don't know how Italians would initially feel about this take on biscotti, but I'm pretty sure that just one bite would win them over! If you find Skor bits in your biscotti a little radical, you can easily change it up to suit your tastes—dried cherries, toasted almonds or pistachios are all delicious options.

Double Chocolate Toffee Biscotti

2 cups all-purpose flour

⅓ cup dark cocoa

1 ½ teaspoons baking powder

¼ teaspoon salt

1 tablespoon instant espresso powder

2 tablespoons hot water

½ cup butter, room temperature

¾ cup granulated sugar

2 large eggs

¾ cup dark chocolate chips

1 cup Skor bits

EGG WASH

1 large egg

2 tablespoon cold water

Coarse sanding sugar, for sprinkling

FINISHING

1 cup dark chocolate chips

2 Skor bars, crushed

MAKES: 18 biscotti

YOU WILL NEED: cookie sheet lined with parchment paper

1. Preheat the oven to 350°F.

2. Onto a large piece of parchment paper, sift together the flour, cocoa, baking powder and salt. Set aside.

3. In a small bowl, dissolve the espresso powder in the hot water. Set aside.

4. In a stand mixer fitted with a paddle attachment, cream the butter and sugar on medium to high speed until light and fluffy. Scrape down the sides of the bowl. Add the eggs one at a time and beat briefly after each addition. Scrape down the sides of the bowl. Add the espresso.

5. Turn the mixer to low and add the dry ingredients and mix to combine. Add the dark chocolate chips and Skor bits and mix to fully distribute.

6. Place the dough on the prepared cookie sheet and shape into a log, about 18 inches long × 3 inches wide.

7. In a small bowl, whisk together the egg and water to make an egg wash. Use a pastry brush to gently coat the top and the sides of the dough with the wash. Sprinkle with a little sanding sugar.

8. Bake in the preheated oven for 25 to 30 minutes or until the top is firm to the touch and a wooden skewer inserted into the center comes out clean.

9. Remove from the oven and allow to cool on the cookie sheet.

10. Keep the log on the parchment paper and carefully transfer it to a cutting board. Use a serrated knife to cut on the diagonal into 18 even slices. Transfer back to the cookie sheet—still on the parchment paper—and bake in the oven for an additional 8 to 10 minutes.

11. Remove from the oven and allow to cool on the cookie sheet.

12. In a small saucepan over medium-low heat, melt the chocolate chips. Use a small spoon to drizzle the top of each biscotti with melted chocolate. Sprinkle on some crushed Skor bars.

13. Allow the chocolate to set for about 1 hour before serving. You can place the biscotti in the refrigerator to help the chocolate set quicker.

If you do not have any Skor bars on hand, you can substitute chopped nuts, but I honestly think you will be happier if you run to the store and pick some up. Skor bars are what really make this biscotti! It can be kept in an airtight container for at least 1 week.

*T*he rainy season can be long in Vancouver. Sometimes you just need to get away to somewhere tropical, but that isn't always possible. So I came up with these biscotti to help chase the blues away. It may not be a holiday in the sun, but at least you don't have to worry about sand getting in everything as you enjoy them.

Tropical Biscotti

2 cups all-purpose flour

1 ½ teaspoons baking powder

¼ teaspoon salt

½ cup pecans, chopped

½ cup butter, room temperature

¾ cup granulated sugar

2 large eggs

2 tablespoons dark rum

1 cup dried pineapple, chopped into
    ½-inch pieces

½ cup dried apricots, chopped into
    ½-inch pieces

EGG WASH

1 large egg

2 tablespoons cold water

Coarse sanding sugar, for sprinkling

FINISHING

2 cups white chocolate chips

2 tablespoons butter

MAKES: **18 biscotti**

YOU WILL NEED: **cookie sheet lined
    with parchment paper**

1. Preheat the oven to 350°F.

2. Onto a large piece of parchment paper, sift together the flour, baking powder and salt. Set aside.

3. Place the pecans on the cookie sheet and bake in the preheated oven for about 10 minutes or until lightly toasted. Flip the nuts with a metal spatula at the halfway point to ensure even toasting. Remove from the oven and set aside to cool.

4. In a stand mixer fitted with a paddle attachment, cream the butter and sugar on medium to high speed until light and fluffy. Scrape down the sides of the bowl. Add the eggs one at a time and beat briefly after each addition. Scrape down the sides of the bowl and add the dark rum. Scrape down the sides of the bowl again.

5. Turn the mixer to low and add the dry ingredients and mix to combine. Add the pineapple, apricots and pecans and mix to fully distribute.

6. Place the dough on the prepared cookie sheet and shape into a log, about 18 inches long × 3 inches wide.

7. In a small bowl, whisk together the egg and water to make an egg wash. Use a pastry brush to gently coat the top and sides of the dough with the wash. Sprinkle with a little sanding sugar.

8. Bake in the preheated oven for 25 to 30 minutes or until the top is firm to the touch and a wooden skewer inserted into the center comes out clean.

9. Remove from the oven and allow to cool on the cookie sheet.

10. Keep the log on the parchment paper and carefully transfer it to a cutting board. Use a serrated knife to cut on the diagonal into 18 even slices. Transfer back to the cookie sheet—still on the parchment paper—and bake in the oven for an additional 8 to 10 minutes.

11. Remove from the oven and allow to cool on the cookie sheet, then transfer to wire racks. Place the wire racks back on top of the cookie sheet (to catch any drops from the next step).

12. In a small saucepan, melt the white chocolate chips and butter. Dip one end of each biscotti into the white chocolate and then place back on the wire rack to set.

13. Allow the chocolate to set for about 1 hour before serving. You can place the biscotti in the refrigerator to help the chocolate set quicker.

The biscotti can be kept in an airtight container for at least 1 week.

This is one of my favorite cookies at the bakery. Our lovely bakers in the kitchen know my weakness for it. They tuck aside all the end bits when they are cutting the biscotti for me to nibble on. For this I love them and curse them all at the same time.

Orange Pecan Biscotti

2 cups all-purpose flour

1 ½ teaspoons baking powder

¼ teaspoon salt

¾ cup pecans

½ cup butter, room temperature

¾ cup granulated sugar

2 large eggs

Zest of 1 orange

2 tablespoons orange juice, freshly
    squeezed

1 cup dark chocolate chips

EGG WASH

1 large egg

2 tablespoon cold water

Coarse sanding sugar, for sprinkling

MAKES: **18 biscotti**

YOU WILL NEED: **cookie sheet lined
    with parchment paper**

1. Preheat the oven to 350°F.

2. Onto a large piece of parchment paper, sift together the flour, baking powder and salt. Set aside.

3. Place the pecans on the cookie sheet and bake in the preheated oven for about 10 minutes or until lightly toasted. Flip the nuts with a metal spatula at the halfway point to ensure even toasting. Remove from the oven and allow to cool. Use a large knife to roughly chop. Set aside.

4. In a stand mixer fitted with a paddle attachment, cream the butter and the sugar on medium to high speed until light and fluffy. Add the eggs one at a time and beat briefly after each addition. Scrape down the sides of the bowl. Add the orange zest and juice. Scrape down the sides of the bowl.

5. Turn the mixer to low and add the dry ingredients and mix to combine. Add the chocolate chips and chopped pecans and mix to fully distribute.

6. Place the dough on the prepared cookie sheet and shape into a log about 18 inches long × 3 inches wide.

7. In a small bowl, whisk together the egg and water to make an egg wash. Use a pastry brush to gently coat the top and the sides of the dough with the wash. Sprinkle with a little sanding sugar.

8. Bake in the preheated oven for 25 to 30 minutes or until the top is firm to the touch and a wooden skewer inserted into the center comes out clean.

9. Remove from the oven and allow to cool on the cookie sheet.

10. Keep the log on the parchment paper and carefully transfer it to a cutting board. Use a serrated knife to cut the log on the diagonal into 18 even slices. Transfer back to the cookie sheet—still on the parchment paper—and bake in the oven for an additional 8 to 10 minutes.

11. Remove from the oven again and allow the biscotti to cool on the cookie sheet.

The biscotti can be kept in an airtight container for at least 1 week.

Bars and Slices

Chapter 4

The Dunbar
$2.75

The Campfire Bar
(graham cracker crust, chocolate and our
toasted vanilla marshmallows)
2.75

I have to give Paul full credit for coming up with the name of this bar. It must be the lawyer in him, but he always manages to recognize the obvious answers that are staring the rest of us in the face. You see, if you come to town on the hunt for Butter Baked Goods, you will find us on—wait for it—Dunbar Street. I'm so glad the shop isn't located on Old Shoe Leather Road.

The Dunbar

1 ½ cups all-purpose flour

1 teaspoon baking soda

½ teaspoon salt

1 cup butter

1 cup dark brown sugar

1 ¼ cups large-flake rolled oats

¾ cup dark chocolate chips

½ cup pecans, lightly chopped

½ cup unsweetened shredded coconut

¾ cup dulce de leche

MAKES: 12 bars

YOU WILL NEED: (9- × 9-inch) pan buttered and lined with parchment paper (see page 30), small piping bag fitted with a round tip

The bars will keep in an airtight container for at least 1 week or in the freezer for up to 1 month.

1. Preheat the oven to 350°F.

2. Onto a large piece of parchment paper, sift together the flour, baking soda and salt. Set aside.

3. In a stand mixer fitted with a paddle attachment, cream the butter and sugar on medium to high speed until light and fluffy. Scrape down the sides of the bowl.

4. Turn the mixer to low and add the dry ingredients and oats and mix until well combined.

5. Divide the dough into two and press half into the prepared pan firmly and evenly. Sprinkle with the chocolate chips, pecans and coconut.

6. Fill the piping bag with the dulce de leche and pipe it over the chocolate chips, pecans and coconut. Use your hands to break the remaining dough into small chunks and sprinkle over the dulce de leche.

7. Bake in the preheated oven for 25 minutes or until golden brown.

8. Remove from the oven and allow the slab to cool in the pan. Run a small knife along the two edges of the pan that do not have parchment handles. Carefully remove the slab from the pan and cut into approximately 2- × 3-inch bars. Make sure to use at least a 10-inch knife to avoid cutting and dragging the knife across the bars.

*O*kay, I should probably confess to you now that I am not really running a bakery at all, but rather I am conducting a secret study on humanity by recording people's preferences in baked goods. According to my notes, calculations and various pie charts, this is far and away our bestselling bar. I've yet to determine what this says about humans as a whole, but it does indicate that they have great taste.

The Dream Slice

CRUST

1 ½ cups all-purpose flour

1 ½ tablespoons granulated sugar

¾ cup butter, chilled

FILLING

3 tablespoons all-purpose flour

1 teaspoon baking powder

¼ teaspoon salt

2 large eggs

¾ cup dark brown sugar

1 teaspoon pure vanilla

1 cup unsweetened shredded coconut

¾ cup walnuts, chopped

½ cup maraschino cherries, drained and finely chopped

BUTTER CREAM

½ cup butter, room temperature

2 cups icing sugar

½ cup heavy cream

MAKES: **20 bars**

YOU WILL NEED: **(9- × 13-inch) pan buttered and lined with parchment paper (see page 30), pastry cutter**

1. Preheat the oven to 350°F.

2. Prepare the crust: In a medium bowl, combine the flour and granulated sugar. Use a pastry cutter to cut in the chilled butter until loose crumbs form. Press the dough into the prepared pan firmly and evenly.

3. Bake in the preheated oven for 10 to 12 minutes or until lightly golden brown.

4. Meanwhile, prepare the filling: Onto a large piece of parchment paper, sift together the flour, baking powder and salt. Set aside.

5. In a stand mixer fitted with a paddle attachment, beat the eggs, brown sugar and vanilla on medium to high speed for 2 to 3 minutes or until pale in color.

6. Turn the mixer to low and add the dry ingredients and mix to combine. Add the coconut, walnuts and cherries and mix until well combined. Spread the filling evenly over the baked crust.

7. Bake for another 25 to 30 minutes or until the filling has set and is lightly browned.

8. Remove from the oven and allow the slab to cool completely in the pan.

9. Meanwhile, prepare the butter cream: In a stand mixer fitted with a paddle attachment, cream the butter and icing sugar on medium to high speed until pale in color. Turn the mixer to low and slowly add the cream. Scrape down the sides of the bowl. Turn the mixer to medium and continue to mix until light and fluffy.

10. Use a small offset spatula to spread the butter cream smoothly overtop the cooled slab. Chill in the refrigerator until the butter cream is firm to the touch.

11. Run a small knife along the two edges of the pan that do not have parchment handles. Carefully remove the slab from the pan and cut into approximately 2- × 2 ¹/₂-inch bars. Make sure to use at least a 10-inch knife to avoid cutting and dragging the knife across the bars.

These bars will keep in an airtight container in the refrigerator for at least 1 week or in the freezer for up to 3 months.

*P*aul says this is the perfect brownie—as long as I don't sprinkle Smarties on it. For such a liberal guy, he has a lot of traditional qualities. I told him to come and join me on the wild side and give the Smarties a chance. If I am feeling a little more serious, I swap out the candy for walnuts.

Smartie Pants Bar

1 cup butter

3 cups bittersweet chocolate chips

6 large eggs

2 cups granulated sugar

1 tablespoon pure vanilla

1 cup all-purpose flour

1 teaspoon salt

1 cup Smarties or 2 cups walnut halves

MAKES: **24 bars**

YOU WILL NEED: **(9- × 13-inch) baking pan buttered and lined with parchment paper (see page 30)**

1. Preheat the oven to 350°F.

2. In a double boiler, or in a heatproof bowl set over a saucepan of simmering water, melt the butter and chocolate and whisk to combine.

3. Transfer to a large bowl and whisk together with the eggs, sugar and vanilla to combine. Add the flour and salt, and whisk to combine.

4. Pour the mixture into the prepared pan and sprinkle evenly with Smarties or walnuts.

5. Bake in the preheated oven for 25 to 30 minutes or until the brownie has puffed up and cracked. This is a very fudgy brownie: It will ultimately fall after being removed from the oven, to create a dense bar.

6. Remove from the oven and allow the slab to cool completely.

7. Run a small knife along the two edges of the pan that do not have parchment handles. Carefully remove the slab from the pan and cut into approximately 2- × 2-inch bars. Make sure to use at least a 10-inch knife to avoid cutting and dragging the knife across the bars.

These bars will keep in an airtight container for up to 1 week or in the freezer for up to 3 months.

I must admit, I am not one for camping. I came up with this bar so that I could enjoy the best part of the trip without leaving the house.

The Campfire Bar

Butter's Famous Vanilla
  Marshmallows (page 227)

¾ cup butter

2 cups graham crumbs

1 300 mL can condensed milk (about
  1 ¼ cups)

¾ cup dark chocolate chips

MAKES: 24 bars

YOU WILL NEED: (9- × 13-inch) baking
  pan buttered and lined with
  parchment paper (see page 30),
  kitchen blowtorch

BEFORE YOU BEGIN: Prepare to Step 4 of Butter's Famous Vanilla Marshmallows (page 227)

1. Preheat the oven to 350°F.

2. In a small saucepan over low heat, melt the butter (or melt in the microwave for about 30 seconds on high). Set aside to cool.

3. In a medium bowl, use a spatula or large spoon to combine the graham crumbs and melted butter. Press the mixture into the prepared pan firmly and evenly to create the base for the bars.

4. In a double boiler, or in a heatproof bowl set over a saucepan of simmering water, melt the chocolate chips. Whisk together the condensed milk and melted chocolate until well combined. Pour the mixture evenly over the graham crumb base.

5. Bake in the preheated oven for 15 minutes or until the chocolate has set.

6. Remove from the oven and allow the slab to cool.

7. Spread the prepared marshmallow evenly overtop the cooled base. Grease a large piece of plastic wrap with butter and lay it directly on top of the marshmallow. Press firmly to flatten and smooth the plastic wrap to cover the marshmallow tightly. Allow to set at room temperature for at least 3 hours or, even better, overnight.

8. Once the marshmallow has set, run a small knife along the two edges of the pan that do not have parchment handles. Carefully remove the slab from the pan. Then gently remove the plastic wrap.

9. Allow the marshmallow to cool, then cut the slab into approximately 2- × 2-inch bars. Make sure to use at least a 10-inch knife to avoid cutting and dragging the knife across the bars.

10. Use a kitchen blowtorch to carefully brown and toast the marshmallow top of each bar to create a true campfire effect. Hold the blowtorch at least 3 inches from the top of the marshmallow and keep it moving back and forth. If you hold the torch too close or for too long in one spot, you run the risk of melting the top of the bars.

I use store-bought graham crumbs for this recipe as they have a nice fine crumb. They are also much easier than crushing loads of crackers in the blender or food processor.

These bars will keep in an airtight container for up to 1 week or in the freezer for up to 3 months.

*W*hat is the quickest way to spot a tourist in Butter? Look for the quizzical expression on their face as they wonder aloud what a *naa-ni-moo* bar is. Understandably so, given that this bar was created in Nanaimo, British Columbia, sometime in the 1950s. Making it a sort of secret Canadian-baked-goods handshake.

The Nanaimo Bar

BASE

2 cups graham crumbs

1 cup unsweetened shredded coconut

½ cup walnuts, chopped

½ cup dark chocolate chips

½ cup plus 1 tablespoon butter

¼ cup granulated sugar

¼ cup dark cocoa

1 large egg

1 teaspoon pure vanilla

FILLING

½ cup butter, room temperature

2 cups icing sugar

1 tablespoon custard powder

2 tablespoons hot water

MAKES: **16 bars**

YOU WILL NEED: (9- × 9-inch) pan buttered and lined with parchment paper (see page 30)

1. In a large bowl, combine the graham crumbs, coconut, walnuts and chocolate chips.

2. In a medium-sized saucepan over medium heat, warm the ½ cup of butter with the sugar and cocoa until the butter is melted and the sugar has dissolved. Allow to cool for a couple of minutes, then add the egg and vanilla and whisk to combine.

3. Pour the melted mixture over the graham crumb mixture and stir until well combined. Press into the prepared pan firmly and evenly. Set aside.

4. Prepare the filling: In a stand mixer fitted with a paddle attachment, cream the butter, icing sugar and custard powder on medium to high speed until pale in color. Scrape down the sides of the bowl and add the hot water. Turn the mixer to medium and continue to beat until the filling is light and fluffy.

5. Use a small offset spatula to spread the filling across the top of the graham crumb base smoothly and evenly. Set aside.

6. In a double boiler, or in a heatproof bowl set over a saucepan of simmering water, melt the chocolate chips and remaining 1 tablespoon of butter. Pour over the filling and spread evenly with the back of a spoon or a small offset spatula. Tap the pan on the countertop to help smooth the chocolate layer.

7. Place the pan in the refrigerator for at least 1 hour or until the chocolate top has set.

8. Run a small knife along the two edges of the pan that do not have parchment handles. Carefully remove the slab from the pan and cut into approximately 2- × 2-inch bars. Make sure to use at least a 10-inch knife to avoid cutting and dragging the knife across the bars.

These bars will keep in an airtight container in the refrigerator for at least 1 week or in the freezer for up to 3 months.

*T*his one is just as fun to say as it is to eat. Trust me when I tell you that it's insanely good. Unless you don't like peanut butter and chocolate. Then it's bloody awful.

Vunderbar

4 cups chocolate wafer crumbs

2 ½ cups icing sugar

2 cups Rice Krispies

1 cup large-flake rolled oats

½ teaspoon salt

3 ½ cups smooth peanut butter

¾ cup butter

1 cup dark chocolate chips

FINISHING

¼ cup milk chocolate chips

¼ cup smooth peanut butter

MAKES: 24 bars

YOU WILL NEED: (9- × 9-inch) baking pan buttered and lined with parchment paper (see page 30), small piping bag fitted with a small round tip (optional)

These bars will keep in an airtight container in the refrigerator for at least 2 weeks or in the freezer for up to 3 months.

1. In a large bowl, combine the chocolate wafer crumbs, icing sugar, Rice Krispies, oats and salt. Set aside.

2. In a double boiler, or in a heatproof bowl set over a saucepan of simmering water, melt the peanut butter and butter. Pour over the chocolate crumb mixture. Use a spatula or large spoon to mix until well combined. Press the mixture into the prepared pan firmly and evenly. Smooth the top with a bench scraper or offset spatula.

3. In a double boiler, or in a heatproof bowl set over a saucepan of simmering water, melt the dark chocolate chips. Pour over the base and spread evenly. Tap the pan on the countertop to help smooth and level it. Place the pan in the refrigerator to chill.

4. In two separate saucepans over low heat or in two separate bowls in the microwave for 20 to 30 seconds, melt the milk chocolate chips and ¼ cup peanut butter.

5. Remove the pan from the refrigerator and use a small spoon, or the small piping bag to drizzle the melted chocolate over the chocolate layer in a haphazard fashion—have some fun with it! Then repeat with the melted peanut butter.

6. Refrigerate for at least 2 hours, or overnight.

7. Run a small knife along the two edges of the pan that do not have parchment handles. Carefully remove the slab from the pan and cut into approximately 2- × 1-inch bars. Make sure to use at least a 10-inch knife to avoid cutting and dragging the knife across the bars.

This is one of those treats that has few ingredients, doesn't require an oven and is weirdly delicious. Traditionally, this was a bar I made only at Christmas. But then that first January at Butter, when it was nowhere to be found, there was some serious feedback from the other side of the counter! We aim to please, so it quickly became a year-round staple in our lineup.

Peanut Butter Marshmallow Slice

Butter's Famous Vanilla
   Marshmallows (page 227)

2 cups butterscotch chips

1 cup peanut butter

½ cup butter

MAKES: **24 slices**

YOU WILL NEED: **(9- × 9-inch) pan buttered and lined with parchment paper (see page 30)**

BEFORE YOU BEGIN: **Prepare a batch of Butter's Famous Vanilla Marshmallows (page 227)**

1. Place the cut marshmallows in a large, wide-mouthed mixing bowl and set aside.

2. In a medium saucepan over medium heat, melt the butterscotch chips, peanut butter and butter. Stir to fully combine.

3. Allow the mixture to cool slightly, then pour it over the marshmallows. Use a spatula or large spoon to gently fold the marshmallows into the peanut butter mixture until they are fully coated.

4. Spread the marshmallows into the prepared pan and give the pan a shake to help settle them. Refrigerate for at least 1 hour, until the mixture has fully set.

5. Run a small knife along the two edges of the pan that do not have parchment handles. Carefully remove the slab from the pan and cut into approximately 2- × 2-inch bars. Make sure to use at least a 10-inch knife to avoid cutting and dragging the knife across the bars.

Instead of making Butter's Famous Marshmallows, you could substitute 4 cups of store-bought marshmallows—but you would be crazy to do so! These bars will keep in an airtight container in the refrigerator for at least 2 weeks or in the freezer for up to 3 months.

*T*his bar is a fun take on the traditional Rice Krispies Treat. They set up nice and firm, which makes them great travelers. Perfect for kids' lunches or as a little something to stash in the bottom of your bag. And what could be better than rooting around in your handbag, searching for your car keys, only to discover a Butterscotch Crispy Bar?

Butterscotch Crispy Bar

8 cups Rice Krispies

1 cup dark brown sugar

1 cup dark corn syrup

1 cup plus 1 tablespoon butter

2 ¼ cups butterscotch chips

1 cup dark chocolate chips

MAKES: **32 bars**

YOU WILL NEED: **(9- × 9-inch) pan buttered and lined with parchment paper (see page 30), small piping bag fitted with a small round tip (optional)**

These bars will keep in an airtight container for at least 1 week or in the freezer for up to 3 months.

1. Place the Rice Krispies in a large mixing bowl and set aside.

2. In a medium saucepan over medium-high heat, combine the sugar, corn syrup and 1 cup of the butter. Bring to a boil and then remove the pan from the heat. Add 2 cups of the butterscotch chips and stir until completely melted.

3. Pour the butterscotch mixture over the Rice Krispies and mix well. Press the cereal mixture into the prepared pan firmly and evenly. Set aside.

4. In a double boiler, or in a heatproof bowl set over a saucepan of simmering water, melt the dark chocolate chips and remaining 1 tablespoon of butter. Pour over the cereal base and spread evenly with the back of a spoon or a small offset spatula.

5. In a double boiler, or in a heatproof bowl set over a saucepan of simmering water, melt the remaining ¼ cup of butterscotch chips. Use a small spoon, or the small piping bag to drizzle the melted butterscotch chips back and forth over the chocolate layer.

6. Chill in the refrigerator for 1 hour or until the chocolate has set.

7. Run a small knife along the two edges of the pan that do not have parchment handles. Carefully remove the slab from the pan and cut into approximately 1- × 2-inch bars. Make sure to use at least a 10-inch knife to avoid cutting and dragging the knife across the bars.

*A*ny day when I can come up with another way to incorporate butterscotch chips into a recipe is a good day. It was an especially good day when I came up with this recipe.

Butterscotch Walnut Bar

BASE

½ cup butter

⅓ cup dark brown sugar

1 ¼ cups all-purpose flour

BATTER

¼ cup butter

2 large eggs

1 cup dark brown sugar

1 teaspoon pure vanilla

1 teaspoon all-purpose flour

½ teaspoon baking powder

¼ teaspoon salt

1 ½ cups walnuts, chopped

¾ cup butterscotch chips

MAKES: **16 bars**

YOU WILL NEED: (9- × 9-inch) pan buttered and lined with parchment paper (see page 30)

These bars will keep in an airtight container for up to 1 week or in the freezer for up to 3 months.

1. Preheat the oven to 350°F.

2. In a stand mixer fitted with a paddle attachment, cream the butter and brown sugar on medium to high speed until light and fluffy. Scrape down the sides of the bowl and add the flour. Mix until combined into a dough. Press the dough into the prepared pan firmly and evenly.

3. Bake in the preheated oven for 10 minutes or until light golden brown in color.

4. Remove from the oven and set aside.

5. Meanwhile prepare the batter: In a small saucepan over low heat, melt the butter (or melt in the microwave for about 30 seconds on high).

6. In a large mixing bowl, whisk together the eggs, sugar, melted butter, vanilla, flour, baking powder and salt until fully combined. Stir in the walnuts and butterscotch chips. Pour the batter evenly over the base.

7. Bake in the preheated oven for 25 minutes or until the center is firm and the top a nice golden brown.

8. Remove from the oven and allow to cool completely in the pan.

9. Run a small knife along the two edges of the pan that do not have parchment handles. Carefully remove the slab from the pan and cut into approximately 2- × 2-inch bars. Make sure to use at least a 10-inch knife to avoid cutting and dragging the knife across the bars.

ondensed milk plays a big part in many of the old recipes that comprise Butter's hit list. Do you think they gave a Nobel Prize to the person who invented condensed milk? If not, they should have.

Lemon Walnut Bar

½ cup butter

1 cup large-flake rolled oats

1 cup all-purpose flour

¾ cup dark brown sugar

½ cup unsweetened shredded coconut

½ cup ground walnuts

1 teaspoon baking powder

1 300 mL can condensed milk (about 1 ¼ cups)

½ cup lemon juice, freshly squeezed (about 2 lemons)

MAKES: 16 bars

YOU WILL NEED: (9- × 9-inch) pan buttered and lined with parchment paper (see page 30)

These bars will keep in an airtight container in the refrigerator for at least 1 week or in the freezer for up to 3 months.

1. Preheat the oven to 350°F.

2. In a small saucepan over low heat, melt the butter (or melt in the microwave for about 30 seconds on high).

3. In a large bowl, combine the oats, flour, sugar, coconut, ground walnuts and baking powder. Pour in the melted butter and mix with a spatula or large spoon until the butter is evenly distributed. Press half the oat mixture into the prepared pan firmly and evenly.

4. In a medium mixing bowl, whisk together the condensed milk and lemon juice until fully combined and slightly thickened. Pour the lemon mixture over the base. Use the back of a spoon or a small offset spatula to spread the filling evenly across the base. Sprinkle the remaining half of the oat mixture over the filling.

5. Bake in the preheated oven for 22 to 25 minutes or until the top is a golden brown.

6. Remove from the oven and allow to cool completely in the pan.

7. Run a small knife along the two edges of the pan that do not have parchment handles. Carefully remove the slabs from the pan and cut into approximately 2- × 2-inch bars. Make sure to use at least a 10-inch knife to avoid cutting and dragging the knife across the bars.

This might be the oldest bar recipe in the bakery. Every customer seems to have a great aunt or grandmother who used to make them. Everyone knows it and loves it! The recipe couldn't be simpler thanks to the special magic of condensed milk, so if you are tight for time, this is the bar to make.

Hey There, Doll Face!

¾ cup pecans

½ cup butter

1 ¼ cups graham crumbs

¾ cup condensed milk

1 cup dark chocolate chips

¾ cup sweetened fancy long shred coconut

MAKES: **16 bars**

YOU WILL NEED: **cookie sheet, (9- × 9-inch) pan buttered and lined with parchment paper (see page 30)**

The bars will keep in an airtight container for up to 1 week or in the freezer for up to 3 months.

1. Preheat the oven to 350°F.

2. Place the pecans on a cookie sheet and bake in the preheated oven for about 10 minutes or until lightly toasted. Flip the nuts with a metal spatula at the halfway point to ensure even toasting. Remove from the oven and allow to cool. Lightly chop and then set aside.

3. In a small saucepan over low heat, melt the butter (or melt in the microwave for about 30 seconds on high).

4. Place the graham crumbs in a large bowl and pour the melted butter on top. Mix well to fully combine. Press the graham crumb mixture into the prepared pan firmly and evenly. Use the back of a spoon or a small offset spatula to spread the condensed milk over the graham crumb base.

5. In another bowl, mix together the toasted pecans, chocolate chips and coconut. Sprinkle over the condensed milk.

6. Bake in the preheated oven for 15 to 17 minutes or until the coconut is just lightly browned.

7. Remove from the oven and allow to cool completely in the pan.

8. Run a small knife along the two edges of the pan that do not have parchment handles. Carefully remove the slab from the pan and cut into approximately 2- × 2-inch bars. Make sure to use at least a 10-inch knife to avoid cutting and dragging the knife across the bars.

This is the closest we come to making cheesecake at Butter, as I am not a huge fan of baked cheesecakes. I am, however, a pretty big fan of this bar. I think the ratio of cheesecake filling to chocolate base is bang on, and the fresh seasonal berries help rationalize my indulgence.

Chocolate Berry Cheesecake Bar

1 cup butter, room temperature

1 ½ cups icing sugar

2 cups all-purpose flour

½ cup dark cocoa

1 8-ounce package cream cheese

1 300-mL can of condensed milk
(about 1 ¼ cups)

1 large egg

1 tablespoon pure vanilla

2 cups mixed blueberries,
raspberries and blackberries

MAKES: 24 bars

YOU WILL NEED: (9- × 13-inch) baking pan buttered and lined with parchment paper (see page 30)

These bars will keep in an airtight container in the refrigerator for up to 1 week or in the freezer for up to 3 months.

1. Preheat the oven to 350°F.

2. In a stand mixer fitted with a paddle attachment, cream the butter and icing sugar on medium to high until light and fluffy. Scrape down the sides of the bowl.

3. Turn the mixer to low and add the flour and cocoa and mix until well combined. Spread two-thirds of the mixture into the prepared pan and press down firmly and evenly.

4. Bake in the preheated oven for 15 minutes.

5. Remove from the oven and set aside.

6. Meanwhile, in a stand mixer fitted with a paddle attachment, whip the cream cheese, condensed milk, egg and vanilla on medium speed until thick and creamy. Pour the mixture evenly over the cooled chocolate base and then sprinkle with the berries. Sprinkle the reserved one-third of the base mixture evenly over the berries.

7. Bake in the preheated oven for about 25 minutes or until the cheesecake layer has set. (It will firm up even more as it cools.)

8. Remove from the oven and allow to cool completely in the pan.

9. Run a small knife along the two edges of the pan that do not have parchment handles. Carefully remove the slab from the pan and cut into approximately 2- × 2-inch bars. Make sure to use at least a 10-inch knife to avoid cutting and dragging the knife across the bars.

As our first Easter at Butter approached, the grocery stores were asking if we had anything special on offer. Trying to think fast, I came up with the idea of a toasted coconut marshmallow Easter Bunny. When the Easter Bunnies were cut out of the pan of marshmallow, we were left with all the extra bits of marshmallow from around the edges and the in-between. A voice in my head started chanting, "Waste not, want not," and I quickly created this bar.

Marshmallow Bunny Bits Brownies

½ batch Butter's Famous Toasted Coconut Marshmallows (page 229)

1 cup dark brown sugar

1 large egg

½ cup all-purpose flour

½ cup whole milk

1 teaspoon pure vanilla

½ cup butter

½ cup dark cocoa

1 ⅔ cups dark chocolate chips

1 cup walnuts, chopped

MAKES: 16 bars

YOU WILL NEED: (9- × 9-inch) pan buttered and lined with parchment paper (see page 30)

BEFORE YOU BEGIN: Prepare a batch of Butter's Famous Toasted Coconut Marshmallows (page 229). You only need half the batch so will have lots left over.

1. Preheat the oven to 350°F.

2. In a large mixing bowl, combine the sugar, egg, flour, milk and vanilla. Set aside.

3. In a medium saucepan over low heat, melt the butter. Add the cocoa and whisk to fully combine.

4. Pour the cocoa mixture over the ingredients in the mixing bowl and whisk to combine. Spread the mixture into the prepared pan to create the base for the bars.

5. Bake in the preheated oven for 20 minutes or until it has set.

6. Remove from the oven and sprinkle the base with the chocolate chips and walnuts. Return the pan to the oven for about 5 minutes or until the chocolate chips start to melt.

7. Remove from the oven again and sprinkle the marshmallows over the melted chocolate chips. Press them lightly with the palms of your hands to help them adhere to the chocolate. Allow to cool completely in the pan.

8. Run a small knife along the two edges of the pan that do not have parchment handles. Carefully remove the slab from the pan and cut into approximately 2- × 2-inch bars. Make sure to use at least a 10-inch knife to avoid cutting and dragging the knife across the bars.

This recipe requires only half the quantity of Butter's Famous Toasted Coconut Marshmallows recipe. The other half will keep in an airtight container for up to 3 months for you to ration as you see fit. The bars themselves will keep in an airtight container for at least 1 week or in the freezer for up to 3 months.

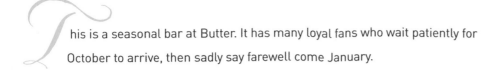

This is a seasonal bar at Butter. It has many loyal fans who wait patiently for October to arrive, then sadly say farewell come January.

Pumpkin Chocolate Chip Blondies

2 ½ cups all-purpose flour

2 tablespoons pumpkin pie spice

1 ½ teaspoons baking soda

1 teaspoon salt

1 cup butter

1 ¾ cups granulated sugar

1 large egg

1 ½ cups pumpkin puree

2 tablespoons pure vanilla

1 ½ cups dark chocolate chips

MAKES: **24 bars**

YOU WILL NEED: **(9- × 13-inch) baking pan buttered and lined with parchment paper (see page 30)**

1. Preheat the oven to 350°F.

2. Onto a large piece of parchment paper, sift together the flour, pumpkin pie spice, baking soda and salt. Set aside.

3. In a stand mixer fitted with a paddle attachment, beat the butter on medium speed. Add the sugar and beat until light and fluffy. Add the egg, pumpkin puree and vanilla and beat until fully combined. Scrape down the sides of the bowl.

4. Turn the mixer to low and add the dry ingredients and mix until fully combined. Fold in the chocolate chips. Spread the batter evenly into the prepared pan and smooth the top with a small offset spatula or the back of a large spoon.

5. Bake in the preheated oven for 35 to 40 minutes or until a wooden skewer inserted in the center comes out clean.

6. Remove from the oven and allow to cool completely in the pan.

7. Run a small knife along the two edges of the pan that do not have parchment handles. Carefully remove the slab from the pan and cut into approximately 2- × 2-inch bars. Make sure to use at least a 10-inch knife to avoid cutting and dragging the knife across the bars.

These bars will keep in an airtight container for up to 5 days or in the freezer for up to 3 weeks.

Butter Creams and Frostings

Chapter 5

A really good butter cream is a magical thing. The secret, of course, lies in using lots of butter, less icing sugar and a good mixer. At the bakery we are really fortunate to have powerful mixers, which help create the light and fluffy butter cream we are known for. The same results are possible at home with your stand mixer by making sure your butter is not too cold, and then whipping it like crazy! The fluffier and lighter your butter cream, the easier it is to work with when frosting a cake.

Butter's Famous Butter Cream

2 cups butter, room temperature

4 cups icing sugar, sifted

½ cup whole milk

2 tablespoons pure vanilla

MAKES: **4 cups, enough for 1 (7-inch) cake or 18 cupcakes**

1. In a stand mixer fitted with a paddle attachment, beat the butter on high speed until very pale in color. Stop the mixer and scrape down the sides of the bowl at least twice while beating the butter.

The next step is very important—we have had a few bakers who have forgotten, from time to time, to reduce the mixer speed before adding the sugar. Trust me when I tell you, pouring icing sugar into a mixer on high speed creates one heck of a mess!

2. Turn the mixer to low and slowly add the icing sugar. Mix until well combined and then slowly add the milk and vanilla. Scrape down the sides of the bowl.

3. Turn the mixer to high and let it run for at least 10 to 12 minutes, until the butter cream is light and fluffy.

BEYOND VANILLA

Straight-up Vanilla Butter Cream is pretty fantastic, but there are plenty more options to try. If you would like to experiment, add the colorings or flavorings listed on the next page to the butter cream after Step 3 of the recipe. Give a few more turns in the mixer to combine.

Butter Cream Variations

MINT BUTTER CREAM

1 teaspoon of mint extract and a splash of green food coloring

PISTACHIO BUTTER CREAM

2 tablespoons of pistachio paste

HAZELNUT BUTTER CREAM

2 tablespoons of hazelnut paste

COFFEE BUTTER CREAM

1 tablespoon of coffee liqueur

RASPBERRY BUTTER CREAM

2 tablespoons of raspberry puree (recipe included with Raspberry Marshmallows, see page 229)

Deep Dark Chocolate Butter Cream

1 cup butter, room temperature

1 cup dark chocolate chips

3 cups icing sugar

¾ cup dark cocoa

½ cup whole milk

MAKES: **4 cups, enough for 1 (7-inch) cake or 18 cupcakes**

1. In a stand mixer fitted with a paddle attachment, beat the butter on high speed until very pale in color. Stop the mixer and scrape down the sides of the bowl at least twice while beating the butter.

2. In a double boiler, or in a heatproof bowl set over a saucepan of simmering water, melt the chocolate chips until smooth. Set aside to cool slightly.

3. Onto a large piece of parchment paper, sift together the icing sugar and cocoa.

4. Turn the mixer to low and slowly add the dry ingredients to the creamed butter. Mix until well combined. Scrape down the sides of the bowl. Slowly add the melted chocolate. Scrape down the sides of the bowl. Slowly add the milk. Scrape down the sides of the bowl again.

5. Turn the mixer to high and let it run for at least 10 to 12 minutes, until the butter cream is light and fluffy.

STORING BUTTER CREAM

You can store all of the butter creams in the refrigerator, in a covered bowl, for at least a week. You just have to soften it up by re-whipping when you want to use it next. Allow the chilled butter cream to come to room temperature first, then mix it in the stand mixer until it is once again light and fluffy (this shouldn't take more than a couple of minutes).

White Chocolate Butter Cream

2 cups butter, room temperature

½ cup white chocolate chips or a
    chunk, chopped

4 cups icing sugar, sifted

½ cup whole milk

2 tablespoons pure vanilla

MAKESL 4 cups, enough for
    1 (7-inch) cake or 18 cupcakes

1. In a stand mixer fitted with a paddle attachment, beat the butter on high speed until very pale in color. Stop the mixer and scrape down the sides of the bowl at least twice while beating the butter.

2. In a double boiler, or in a heatproof bowl set over a saucepan of simmering water, melt the chocolate until smooth. Set aside to cool slightly.

3. Turn the mixer to low and slowly add the icing sugar. Mix until well combined then slowly add the milk and vanilla. Scrape down the sides of the bowl.

4. Turn the mixer to high and let it run for at least 10 to 12 minutes, until the butter cream is light and fluffy.

5. Remove the bowl from the mixer stand and use a small spatula to gently fold in the melted chocolate until fully incorporated.

Lemon Butter Cream

2 cups butter, room temperature

4 cups icing sugar, sifted

½ cup whole milk

Zest of 1 lemon

2 tablespoons lemon juice

1 drop yellow food coloring (optional,
    to give to a soft lemony color)

MAKES: 4 cups, enough for
    1 (7-inch) cake or 18 cupcakes

1. In a stand mixer fitted with a paddle attachment, beat the butter on high speed until very pale in color. Stop the mixer and scrape down the sides of the bowl at least twice while beating the butter.

2. Turn the mixer to low and slowly add the icing sugar. Mix until well combined then slowly add the milk, lemon zest, lemon juice and food coloring (if using). Scrape down the sides of the bowl again.

3. Turn the mixer to high and let it run for at least 10 to 12 minutes, until the butter cream is light and fluffy.

Peanut Butter Butter Cream

1 ½ cups smooth peanut butter

½ cup butter, room temperature

4 cups icing sugar, sifted

1 cup heavy cream

MAKES: 4 cups, enough for
1 (7-inch) cake or 18 cupcakes

1. In a stand mixer fitted with a paddle attachment, beat the peanut butter and butter on high speed until very pale in color. Scrape down the sides of the bowl at least twice while beating the butter.

2. Turn the mixer to low and slowly add the icing sugar. Mix until well combined then slowly add the cream. Scrape down the sides of the bowl again.

3. Turn the mixer to high and let it run for at least 10 to 12 minutes, until the butter cream is light and fluffy.

Cream Cheese Butter Cream

1 ½ cups butter, room temperature

½ cup cream cheese, room temperature

4 cups icing sugar

½ cup whole milk

2 tablespoons pure vanilla

MAKES: 4 cups, enough for
1 (7-inch) cake or 18 cupcakes

1. In a stand mixer fitted with a paddle attachment, beat the butter and cream cheese on high speed until very pale in color. Scrape down the sides of the bowl at least twice while beating to make sure the butter and cream cheese are evenly combined.

2. Turn the mixer to low and slowly add the icing sugar. Mix until well combined then slowly add the milk and vanilla. Scrape down the sides of the bowl again.

3. Turn the mixer to high and let it run for at least 10 to 12 minutes, until the butter cream is light and fluffy.

*T*his is the icing we use on all of Butter's Shaped Cookies (page 84). You control the thickness of the icing simply by altering the amount of water you add. Go light on the water to begin with, as even food coloring will thin the icing.

Royal Icing

4 cups icing sugar

¼ cup meringue powder

6 to 8 tablespoons water

MAKES: 4 cups, enough to coat about 24 cookies

1. In a stand mixer fitted with a whisk attachment, combine the icing sugar and meringue powder. Mix on medium speed until the meringue powder is evenly distributed throughout the icing sugar.

2. Turn the mixer to low and slowly add the water, little by little, until the icing reaches the desired thickness and consistency (see the note below).

3. Once the water is incorporated, beat the mixture on high to create some volume and lightness in the icing.

CONSISTENCY AND COLOR

When icing cookies, you need two different consistencies of icing. The "dam" icing should be thick enough to hold its shape; the "flood" icing should be loose enough to spread across a cookie without being so thin that it runs off (see page 142). Royal Icing can become any shade you like just by adding a drop of food coloring. The combination of meringue powder and icing sugar gives it a pure white base that means all colors read true when tinting, so show restraint when you start adding the coloring. You know the phrase "you can't put the toothpaste back in the tube"? Well the same goes for food coloring. One drop too many and your pale pastel yellow will be a shade better suited for school buses! Add one drop at a time, and mix well between each addition, until you reach the depth of color you want.

B oiled icing (or Marshmallow Fluff Frosting as we like to call it at Butter) is one of life's great mysteries, until you discover how easy it is to make. All you need is a candy thermometer and you're away to the races!

Marshmallow Fluff Frosting

2 cups granulated sugar

¼ cup water

2 tablespoons light corn syrup

6 egg whites (see page 26)

MAKES: **4 cups, enough for 1 (7-inch) cake or 18 cupcakes**

YOU WILL NEED: **pastry brush, candy thermometer**

This icing is best used right away, as it won't spread as nicely once it has cooled.

1. In a small saucepan over medium heat, combine 1 ½ cups of the sugar with the water and corn syrup. Stir until the sugar has dissolved. Increase heat to high and bring to a boil.

2. Wash down the sides of the pan with a wet pastry brush to remove any sugar crystals. Measure the temperature with the candy thermometer and continue to boil until it reaches 230°F.

3. In a stand mixer fitted with a whisk attachment, beat the egg whites on high speed until soft peaks form. Turn the mixer to medium and gradually add the remaining ½ cup of sugar, 1 tablespoon at a time.

4. Turn the mixer to low and slowly add the hot sugar mixture, pouring it in a steady stream down the side of the bowl. Let the mixer run until the frosting is cool and thick and shiny.

T his glaze couldn't be easier to make or more delicious to eat. Always try to use the best chocolate you can find, for tastiest results.

Chocolate Glaze

2 cups chocolate chips

2 tablespoons butter

MAKES: **2 cups, enough for 1 (9-inch) cake or 18 cupcakes**

1. In a double boiler, or in a heatproof bowl set over a saucepan of simmering water, melt the chocolate chips and butter until very thin and smooth. Whisk to combine as they melt.

2. Remove from the heat and allow to cool slightly before use.

Icing Techniques

I thought now might be a good time to talk a little about icing techniques. At Butter we are known for our delicious Butter Cream and our simple and honest approach to applying it. Somehow I just don't find food as appealing if it looks as though it has been fussed and mussed with too much. On the pages ahead you will find some really simple tips to follow when icing the cakes and cupcakes in the next two chapters.

PRACTICE

There is only one important thing to remember about icing. Just like learning any skill, it is all about practice, practice, practice! The cakes and cupcakes I iced when I opened the bakery look a far cry different from those I ice today (and a big thank-you to everyone for being so patient with me).

Using a piping bag or offset spatula may feel awkward at first, but stick with it because once you get the hang of it, your cakes and cup-cakes will take on a professional look. Use a piece of parchment paper to practice icing and frosting with the various shapes and sizes of piping tips. Soon your friends and family will start asking which bakery you shop at!

Preparing Piping Bags

FILLING A PIPING BAG

Like most things in life, and all things in icing, filling a piping bag gets easier the more often you do it—which is a great excuse to put icing on everything!

1. Attach the piping tip to the piping bag; give the bag a little twist above the piping tip to prevent the icing from running right through.

2. Fold back the top of the bag about halfway, this creates a cuff to place your hand under when holding the bag with one hand and filling it with the other. Alternatively, rest the piping bag in a liquid measuring cup while filling it, if one-handedness proves too tricky. Use a large spatula to scoop the icing into the bag and fill it about halfway full.

3. Unroll the cuff and use a bench scraper to push the filling to the bottom of the bag to remove any air pockets. Untwist the end of the bag at this stage, then twist the top of the bag several times to force the filling down into the tip. As the bag empties, keep twisting the top of the bag to force the filling down into the tip to create a consistent flow.

MAKING A PAPER CORNET

If you don't have a piping bag on hand, you can create one using parchment paper. This is great for icing cookies and trimming cakes, especially when you want to add a small detail, like a tiny leaf or a little smile on a bumble bee.

1. Trim a sheet of parchment paper to create a square about 12 × 12 inches. Fold the square in half to form a triangle and place it on your work surface with the peak pointing toward you.

2. Take the right-hand point of the triangle and roll it toward you. Pull it tight to get a pointed tip at the center of the flat edge furthest from you. Fold the left side toward you and around the cone, pulling it tight to seal the point. Fold the flaps down into the cone to secure it.

3. Fill the cornet with icing. Flatten the top of the cornet, and fold in the corners, then roll down the top to seal the cornet. Snip the tip to create a small piping opening.

Icing Cookies

Icing cookies can be a lot of fun if you are well prepared and have all the tools on hand. You will need several icing bags fitted with round tips and plenty of Royal Icing (page 136) in a variety of colors and thicknesses. If you are working with multiple colors, separate them into individual bowls and cover the bowls you are not using with a damp paper towel to help keep the moisture in. Icing can dry out very quickly, which can cause nasty little lumps that are hard to get through the tip of the piping bag.

The biggest trick to icing sugar cookies is creating a thicker outline or "dam" around the edge of the cookie first. Then "flood" the center of the cookie with thinner Royal Icing to create a smooth and even coating. If the thinner icing needs a little help making it to the edge of the cookie, use the edge of a wooden skewer or a tiny paintbrush to drag it there. Allow the icing to dry before putting on the next level of detail (this won't take longer than 15 minutes) to prevent the various colors from blending together.

Icing Cupcakes

At Butter we try so many variations of cupcake and frosting flavor combinations, we're spoiled for choice.

CLASSIC

Regardless of the flavor, we ice nearly all our cupcakes using a 14-inch piping bag fitted with a large star tip. It couldn't be simpler or quicker. Hold the piping bag at a sharp angle above the cupcake. Start at the outer edge and slowly and carefully pipe your way around in a circle to the center of the cupcake. When you reach the center, stop piping and pull up quickly to create a little peak of icing at the center.

For a nice finish, top your cupcakes with a decoration to reflect the flavor of the frosting. We top our lemon frosting with a little lemon jelly slice, and our Hazelnut Butter Cream with a sprinkling of crushed hazelnuts. And if all else fails, multicolored sprinkles are always in fashion! A little dusting of them adds just the right amount of whimsy and light heartedness.

ROSE TOP

A fun alternative for finishing cupcakes is to ice the top to look like a very pretty pastel-colored rose. This is a beautiful finish and isn't as tricky as it looks.

Fit one piping bag with a small leaf tip and fill the bag with pale green butter cream. Pipe four little "leaves" on the cupcake at evenly spaced points around the edge. Fit a second piping bag with a large star tip and fill with a pretty pastel-colored butter cream. Hold the bag at a sharp angle above the cupcake and begin to pipe at the center of the cupcake, working outward. Pipe the icing around the top of the cupcake slowly and carefully to create a rose pattern.

Icing Cakes

A rotating cake stand (see page 19) really comes in handy when icing cakes as it allows you to spin the cake while holding an offset spatula in one place. This will result in an even layer of icing across the sides and top. As with a piping bag, this takes practice. But unlike practicing the piano when you were little, this practice is tasty!

CRUMB COAT

The first step to a professional finish on an iced cake is the crumb coat. The crumb coat helps prevent any crumbs from turning up in the top coat and making your masterpiece look messy.

1. Place a small dollop of icing on a cake stand or board (the icing acts like a glue, helping to affix the cake and prevent it from moving around while you are hard at work) and place the first layer of cake on top of it.

2. Use a large offset spatula to spread a generous helping of butter cream smoothly and evenly across the cake layer (a 7-inch cake will use about $1/2$ cup of butter cream between each). Place the second layer of cake on top of the first and repeat the process until all layers are frosted.

3. Use an offset spatula to thinly coat the top and sides with butter cream to seal the whole cake as smoothly as you can.

4. Briefly refrigerate the cake until the icing is nice and firm, no more than 15 minutes. This will help set the crumb coat, which will make the top coat of icing much easier to apply.

TOP COAT

When applying the final coat on any cake, I always start with the sides of the cake and finish with the top, and I always use a large offset spatula for the smoothest of finishes. Once you have a smooth final coat on the cake, you can finish it in a number of ways.

RIBBED SIDES   This is what I used to create the finish on Butter's Chocolate Cake (page 150). To achieve it, run a serrated blade gently around the sides of the cake to create a ribbed pattern. This is best achieved using a rotating cake stand and holding the blade in place on the side of the cake and then slowly spinning the cake stand.

PIPED TOP AND BOTTOM   I like this traditional finish for our classic birthday cakes, whether they're vanilla or chocolate. Put that piping bag to work and pipe the top and base line of the cake with a pretty row of stars or scallops, and then dust the top of the cake with some sprinkles. Both stars and scallops can be achieved with a sure hand and a large star tip fitted to your piping bag. For scallops, pull the piping tip up and away from you and then begin releasing pressure while pulling it towards you, making sure to slightly overlap the last scallop each time. For a star finish, simply hold the bag vertically and squeeze to form a star on the top or sides of the cake, releasing the pressure before lifting up. This may sound a bit challenging but I can assure you it's really simple! If, like me, you are more of a visual learner you can find lots of quick and simple instructional videos online.

ENCRUSTED SIDES   This is the technique I use for our Coconut Cake (page 154) and our Carrot Cake (page 153), but it works just as well on a chocolate cake with mint icing, encrusted with chocolate sprinkles, as shown here. Fill a large bowl with 2-3 cups of the sprinkles or nuts of your choosing. If you have iced your cake on a cake board, carefully balance the board in the palm of one hand and hold it over the bowl. Use your hands to scoop up and gently press handfuls of the nuts or sprinkles onto the sides of the cake. If you have iced your cake on a cake stand, you can place it on a cookie sheet while you encrust the sides. The excess will fall away back into the bowl or onto the cookie sheet, so you can scoop it up and repeat the process until the sides are completely coated.

Cakes

Chapter 6

*F*inding a recipe for a great white cake can be a challenge. I found they were either dense and dry or a bit of sponge fluff with no body. Well, not to worry—the search is over. This cake is the foundation of a variety of different cakes that we make at Butter, including our famously popular Coconut Cake. Master this recipe and you will have a great workhorse for years to come.

Butter's Classic White Cake

2 ¼ cups pastry flour

1 tablespoon baking powder

½ teaspoon salt

½ cup butter, room temperature

1 ½ cups sugar

4 egg whites

½ tablespoon pure vanilla

1 ¼ cups buttermilk

FROSTING
Butter's Famous Butter Cream
    (page 130)

MAKES: 1 cake, about 8 to 12 slices
(or 2 if you are hungry!)

YOU WILL NEED: 2 (7-inch) circular
cake pans buttered and floured

1. Preheat the oven to 350°F.

2. Onto a large piece of parchment paper, sift together the flour, baking powder and salt. Set aside.

3. In a stand mixer fitted with a paddle attachment, beat the butter on medium speed until light and fluffy. Add the sugar, egg whites and vanilla and continue to beat until well combined.

4. Turn the mixer to low and add the dry ingredients and buttermilk alternately (begin and end with the dry). Scrape down the sides of the bowl at least twice during the mixing.

5. Spoon the batter evenly into the prepared pans. Bake in the preheated oven for 25 to 30 minutes or until a wooden skewer inserted into the center comes out clean.

Monitor the cakes carefully as they bake. They are ready when the tops are flat and lightly browned. It's important not to overbake them, as they can become dry and too firm.

6. Meanwhile, prepare Butter's Famous Butter Cream.

7. Remove from the oven and allow to cool for about 10 minutes then invert the cakes onto wire racks to cool completely. You may need to run a sharp knife around the edge of the pan if the cakes do not easily fall when first inverted.

8. Transfer the cakes to a rotating cake stand and use a large serrated knife to cut each cake in half on the horizontal to create four layers. Follow the steps of Icing Cakes (on page 144) to ice the cake in the style of your choice.

Butter's Famous Butter Cream tinted a lovely shade of pale pink is my favorite choice for this cake. If you are in a rush (or things just aren't working out for you today in the kitchen), simply ice between the layers of the cake and on the top. Leave the sides bare and the icing will peek invitingly from between the layers.

I think learning to make a really good chocolate cake is a life skill up there with driving, doing your own laundry and mastering a good handshake. This is a cake with which to recognize life's achievements, celebrate milestones or offer comfort when life goes sideways. It's a cake to share with friends, or to enjoy alone, in silence, on those nights when you can't sleep.

Butter's Chocolate Cake

2 ¾ cups all-purpose flour

2 teaspoons baking soda

½ teaspoon baking powder

½ teaspoon salt

2 cups hot coffee (any blend)

1 cup dark cocoa

2 cups sugar

1 cup vegetable oil

4 large eggs

½ cup buttermilk

1 ½ teaspoons pure vanilla

FROSTING
Deep Dark Chocolate Butter Cream
    (page 133)

MAKES: 1 cake, about 12 to 16 slices

YOU WILL NEED: 2 (9-inch) circular cake pans buttered and floured

1. Preheat the oven to 350°F.

2. Onto a large piece of parchment paper, sift together the flour, baking soda, baking powder and salt. Set aside.

3. In a medium bowl, whisk the hot coffee with the cocoa until smooth. Set aside to cool slightly.

4. In a large bowl, whisk together the sugar, oil, eggs, buttermilk and vanilla. Add the cocoa and coffee and gently whisk to incorporate. Add the dry ingredients and whisk until well combined. Spoon the batter evenly into the prepared pans.

5. Bake in the preheated oven for 30 to 35 minutes or until a wooden skewer inserted into the center comes out clean.

6. Meanwhile, prepare the Deep Dark Chocolate Butter Cream.

7. Remove from the oven and allow to cool for about 10 minutes then invert onto wire racks to cool completely. You may need to run a sharp knife around the edge of the pan if the cakes do not easily fall when first inverted.

8. Transfer the cakes to a rotating cake stand and use a large serrated knife to cut each cake in half on the horizontal, to create four layers. Follow the steps of Icing Cakes (on page 144) to ice the cake with the Deep Dark Chocolate Butter Cream in the style of your choice. Take a moment to congratulate yourself on a job well done, then dig in!

Chocolate is our customers' favorite choice of butter cream for this cake, but raspberry (page 131) or pistachio (page 131) are also delicious options.

FORK

*W*ho doesn't love a good carrot cake? Especially one that is nice and moist, with little bits of pineapple, flecked with coconut and topped with a thick layer of Cream Cheese Butter Cream. Not a bad way to get your veggies.

Butter's Carrot Cake

1 ¾ cups pastry flour

2 teaspoon cinnamon

1 teaspoon pumpkin pie spice

1 teaspoon baking soda

½ teaspoon baking powder

½ teaspoon salt

1 cup granulated sugar

1 cup vegetable oil

2 large eggs

1 ½ cups grated carrots

¾ cup crushed pineapple with juice

½ cup unsweetened shredded
   coconut

½ cup walnuts, chopped

FROSTING

Cream Cheese Butter Cream
   (page 135)

1 cup walnuts, crushed

MAKES: 1 cake, about 8 to 12 slices

YOU WILL NEED: 2 (7-inch) circular
   cake pans buttered and floured

1. Preheat the oven to 350°F.

2. Onto a large piece of parchment paper, sift together the flour, cinnamon, pumpkin pie spice, baking soda, baking powder and salt. Set aside.

3. In a large bowl, whisk together the sugar and vegetable oil. Add the eggs and continue to whisk until the batter is pale in color. Add the carrots, crushed pineapple and pineapple juice and whisk to incorporate.

4. Sprinkle the dry ingredients over the batter and use a rubber spatula or wooden spoon to blend. Stir in the coconut and walnuts. Spoon the batter evenly into the prepared pans.

5. Bake in the preheated oven for 30 to 35 minutes or until a wooden skewer inserted into the center comes out clean.

6. Meanwhile, prepare the Cream Cheese Butter Cream.

7. Remove from the oven and allow to cool for about 10 minutes then invert onto wire racks to cool completely. You may need to run a sharp knife around the edge of the pan if the cakes do not easily fall when first inverted.

8. Transfer the cakes to a rotating cake stand and use a large serrated knife to cut each cake in half on the horizontal to create four layers. Follow the steps of Icing Cakes (on page 144) to ice the cake with the Cream Cheese Butter Cream. Then take handfuls of the crushed walnuts and press lightly onto the sides of the cake (for tips on Encrusted Sides see page 145).

This recipe makes a four-layer cake, but the cake in the photo is just three. That's how we make them at the bakery, but I thought you'd appreciate the extra layer at home!

This cake wins the popularity contest at Butter every year. It's a cake that is so good, it make converts out of those crazy coconut naysayers.

Butter's Coconut Cake

1 ½ cups pastry flour

¾ cup coconut flour

1 tablespoon baking powder

½ teaspoon salt

½ cup butter, room temperature

1 ½ cups granulated sugar

4 egg whites

½ tablespoon pure vanilla

¾ cup buttermilk

½ cup coconut milk

FROSTING
**Cream Cheese Butter Cream
(page 135)**

**2 to 3 cups sweetened fancy long
shred coconut**

MAKES: **1 cake, about 8 to 12 slices**

YOU WILL NEED: **2 (7-inch) circular
cake pans buttered and floured**

Coconut flour can be found in grocery stores that sell flour alternatives, but if you're in a pinch, you can substitute it with pastry flour.

1. Preheat the oven to 350°F.

2. Onto a large piece of parchment paper, sift together both flours, baking powder and salt. In a liquid measuring cup, whisk together the buttermilk and coconut milk to combine. Set both aside.

3. In a stand mixer fitted with a paddle attachment, beat the butter on medium speed until light and fluffy. Add the sugar, egg whites and vanilla and continue to beat until well combined. Scrape down the sides of the bowl.

4. Turn the mixer to low and add the dry ingredients and milks alternately (begin and end with the dry). Scrape down the sides of the bowl at least twice during the mixing process. Spoon the batter evenly into the prepared pans.

5. Bake in the preheated oven for 25 to 30 minutes or until a wooden skewer inserted into the center comes out clean.

6. Meanwhile, prepare the Cream Cheese Butter Cream.

7. Remove from the oven and allow to cool for about 10 minutes then invert onto wire racks to cool completely. You may need to run a sharp knife around the edge of the pan if the cakes do not easily fall when first inverted.

8. Transfer the cakes to a rotating cake stand and use a large serrated knife to cut each cake in half on the horizontal to create four layers.

9. In a small bowl, combine 1 to 1 ½ cups Cream Cheese Butter Cream with ½ cup coconut to create the frosting. Follow the steps of Icing Cakes (on page 144) to ice the cake. Then take handfuls of the coconut and press lightly onto the sides and top of the cake (for tips on Encrusted Sides see page 145). Invite your family and friends over and start slicing!

I'm not sure if Nabisco gets to take all the credit for this one, but traditionally their cookies were used to make this cake. Do you think I should call them, to tell them how much better it tastes with homemade chocolate cookies instead?

Cookies and Cream Cake

COOKIES

1 ½ cups butter, room temperature

1 ½ cups icing sugar

2 large eggs

1 teaspoon pure vanilla

3 ½ cups all-purpose flour

¼ cup dark cocoa

½ teaspoon salt

FILLING

4 cups 35% whipping cream

¼ cup granulated sugar

2 tablespoons pure vanilla

MAKES: 1 cake, about 8 to 12 slices

YOU WILL NEED: 2 cookie sheets lined with parchment paper, 1 ½-inch circular cookie cutter, (9-inch) round cake plate

1. In a stand mixer fitted with a paddle attachment, cream the butter and icing sugar on medium to high speed until light and fluffy. Add the eggs and vanilla, and mix until combined.

2. Turn the mixer to low and slowly add the flour, cocoa and salt. Increase the speed to medium and mix for 1 minute.

3. Divide the dough in half and shape into two disks, about ½ inch thick each. Wrap each disk in plastic wrap and chill in the refrigerator for at least 60 minutes.

4. Preheat the oven to 325°F.

5. Place one disk of dough on a lightly floured board. Use a rolling pin to roll out to about ¼ inch thick. Use the cookie cutter to cut out about 30 circles. Place on the prepared cookie sheet, about 1 inch apart. Repeat with the second disk of dough.

6. Bake in the preheated oven for about 10 minutes, until just firm to the touch.

7. Meanwhile, prepare the filling: In a stand mixer fitted with a whisk attachment, whip the cream, sugar and vanilla until thick.

8. Remove from the oven and allow the cookies to cool slightly then transfer to wire racks to cool completely.

9. On the cake plate, spread about ½ cup of the whipped cream in an 8-inch circle. Cover the cream with a layer of about 10 cookies, in a circular pattern. Continue to layer the cream and cookies on top of each other until the cake is at least 5 inches high. Finish with a top layer of cream.

10. Refrigerate for at least 2 hours, or overnight, to soften the cookies before serving.

I tend to be a "go big or go home" kind of girl, so when I was creating this lemon cake I made sure to include lemon every step of the way. If you really want to take it over the top, you can add a layer of Lemon Curd (page 205) in addition to Lemon Butter Cream—but then we'd have to call it the Quadruple Lemon Layer Cake!

Triple Lemon Layer Cake

2 ¼ cups pastry flour

1 tablespoon baking powder

½ teaspoon salt

1 ¼ cups whole milk

¼ cup plus 2 tablespoons lemon juice

1 ¾ cups granulated sugar

½ cup butter, room temperature

4 egg whites

½ tablespoon pure vanilla

Zest of 1 lemon

FROSTING

Lemon Butter Cream (page 134)

White sprinkles

MAKES: **1 cake, about 8 to 12 slices**

YOU WILL NEED: **2 (7-inch) circular cake pans buttered and floured**

1. Preheat the oven to 350°F.

2. Onto a large piece of parchment paper, sift together the flour, baking powder and salt. Set aside.

3. Combine the milk and 2 tablespoons of the lemon juice to create a syrup (the milk will curdle, so don't be alarmed). Set aside.

4. In a small saucepan over medium-high heat, combine the remaining ¼ cup of lemon juice and 1½ cups of the sugar, and bring to a boil. Boil for about 1 minute. Remove from the heat and allow to cool slightly.

5. In a stand mixer fitted with a paddle attachment, cream the butter on medium speed, until light and fluffy. Scrape down the sides of the bowl. Add the remaining ¼ cup of sugar, egg whites, vanilla and lemon zest and mix until well combined.

6. Turn the mixer to low and add the dry ingredients and milk alternately (begin and end with the dry). Scrape down the sides of the bowl at least twice during the mixing process. Spoon the batter evenly into the prepared pans.

7. Bake in the preheated oven for 25 to 30 minutes or until a wooden skewer inserted into the center comes out clean. The tops should be flat and lightly browned.

8. Meanwhile, prepare the Lemon Butter Cream.

9. Remove from the oven and allow to cool briefly then invert onto wire racks. You may need to run a sharp knife around the edge of the pan if the cakes do not easily fall when first inverted.

10. Use a wooden skewer to poke small holes all over the bottom of each cake. Use a small pastry brush to coat the bottom of each with the lemon syrup several times. Allow the cakes to cool completely.

11. Place one of the cakes on a cake stand or board, bottom side up. Use an offset spatula to spread a generous helping of Lemon Butter Cream smoothly and evenly across it. Place the second layer on top, bottom side down. Follow the steps of Icing Cakes (page 144) to ice the top and sides. Finish with a light dusting of little white sprinkles.

I don't generally like to play matchmaker, but when I noticed my Apple Cake looking a little lonely, I just knew I had to introduce her to Mr. Maple Sauce. As I suspected, it was love at first sight. But she better watch out because sometimes Mr. Maple Sauce likes to sneak off and mess around with Miss Vanilla Ice Cream . . .

Apple Cake with Maple Sauce

3 cups all-purpose flour

1 ½ teaspoons baking soda

1 ½ teaspoons cinnamon

½ teaspoon nutmeg

½ teaspoon salt

½ cup butter, room temperature

½ cup vegetable oil

1 cup granulated sugar

1 cup light brown sugar

3 large eggs

2 teaspoons pure vanilla

2 large Granny Smith apples, peeled, cored and cut into ½-inch pieces

MAPLE SAUCE

¾ cup pure maple syrup

½ cup butter

½ cup heavy cream

½ teaspoon salt

MAKES: 1 cake, about 12 servings

YOU WILL NEED: (9- × 13-inch) baking pan lightly buttered and floured or lined with parchment paper

1. Preheat the oven to 350°F.

2. Onto a large piece of parchment paper, sift together the flour, baking soda, cinnamon, nutmeg and salt. Set aside.

3. In a stand mixer fitted with a paddle attachment, cream the butter on medium speed for about 2 minutes. Add the oil and mix for another minute. Scrape down the sides of the bowl. Add both sugars and continue to mix until light and fluffy.

4. Add the eggs one at a time and mix well after each addition. Scrape down the sides of the bowl. Add the vanilla and mix to combine. Scrape down the sides of the bowl.

5. Turn the mixer to low and slowly add the dry ingredients until just combined. Remove the bowl from the stand and gently fold in the apple. Spread the batter in the prepared pan.

6. Bake in the preheated oven for about 45 minutes or until golden brown and a wooden skewer inserted into the center comes out clean.

7. Meanwhile, prepare the Maple Sauce: In a small saucepan over medium heat, bring the maple syrup, butter, cream and salt to a boil. Boil for about 1 minute. Remove from the heat and allow to cool slightly.

8. Remove the cake from the oven and allow it to cool slightly. Use a large serrated knife to cut it into 3- × 3-inch squares. Serve warm, with the warm Maple Sauce drizzled on top (and a generous scoop of whipped cream).

You can make the Maple Sauce ahead of time, as it can be stored in the refrigerator for several days. Reheat it before serving in a small saucepan over medium heat.

*N*ever underestimate the power of a bundt pan. As old school as it may seem, some really good things can come out of it. This recipe is for a simple but moist pound cake that few people can resist. It's rich enough that it doesn't need frosting, but a generous helping of Chocolate Glaze (page 137) and a scoop of vanilla ice cream won't hurt.

Chocolate Espresso Pound Cake

3 cups all-purpose flour

½ cup dark cocoa

½ teaspoon baking powder

½ teaspoon salt

1 ½ cups butter at room temperature

1 ½ cups granulated sugar

1 ½ cups light brown sugar

5 large eggs

2 tablespoons instant espresso powder

¼ cup hot water

1 cup milk

1 teaspoon pure vanilla

GLAZE
Chocolate Glaze (page 137)

MAKES: 1 bundt cake, about 10 to 12 slices

YOU WILL NEED: (6-cup) bundt pan buttered and floured, cookie sheet (optional)

1. Preheat the oven to 325°F.

2. Onto a large piece of parchment paper, sift together the flour, cocoa, baking powder and salt. Set aside.

3. In a stand mixer fitted with a paddle attachment, cream the butter and both sugars on medium to high speed until light and fluffy. Add the eggs one at a time and beat well after each addition.

4. In a small bowl, dissolve the espresso powder in the hot water. Stir in the milk and vanilla.

5. Turn the mixer to low and add the dry ingredients alternately with the milk mixture (begin and end with the dry). Scrape down the sides of the bowl after each addition. Pour the batter into the prepared pan.

6. Bake in the preheated oven for 60 minutes or until a wooden skewer inserted into the center comes out clean.

7. Remove from the oven and allow the cake to cool in the pan for at least 10 minutes then transfer to a wire rack to cool completely. Place the wire rack on top of the cookie sheet (to catch any drips when glazing).

8. Meanwhile, prepare the Chocolate Glaze.

9. When the cake has cooled completely, slowly pour the glaze over the top. The glaze will drizzle down the sides of the cake to create a pattern of chocolate stripes. Allow the glaze to set for about 30 minutes at room temperature before serving. (If you are hungry, you can refrigerate the cake to speed up the setting time.)

My daughter, India, loves this cake. And who can blame her? Chocolate, orange, butter . . . what's not to love? I have been told that a slice of this cake is sheer heaven with a big ol' cup of coffee and the Sunday edition of *The New York Times*.

Orange Chocolate Ripple Cake

RIPPLE

½ cup granulated sugar

3 tablespoons dark cocoa

1 tablespoon cinnamon

BATTER

3 cups all-purpose flour

2 teaspoons baking powder

½ teaspoon salt

1 cup butter, room temperature

2 cups granulated sugar

4 large eggs

Zest of 2 oranges

2 cups plain yogurt

2 teaspoons baking soda

ORANGE GLAZE

2 cups icing sugar

¼ cup orange juice, freshly
   squeezed

MAKES: 1 cake, about 10 to 12 slices

YOU WILL NEED: (9-inch) circular
   cake pan, buttered and floured

1. Preheat the oven to 350°F.

2. In a small bowl, combine the ripple ingredients and set aside.

3. Prepare the batter: Onto a large piece of parchment paper, sift together the flour, baking powder and salt. Set aside.

4. In a stand mixer fitted with a paddle attachment, cream the butter on high speed until pale in color. Turn the mixer to medium, slowly add the sugar and beat until light and fluffy. Add the eggs one at a time and beat well after each addition. Scrape down the sides of the bowl after each addition. When the eggs are fully incorporated, add the orange zest.

5. In a medium bowl, mix together the yogurt and baking soda.

6. Turn the mixer to low and add the dry ingredients alternately with the yogurt mixture (begin and end with the dry). Mix on medium-low after each addition. Scrape down the sides of the bowl after each addition. Use the back of a large spoon to spread half the batter evenly in the prepared pan.

7. Sprinkle the ripple mixture on top. Spread the remaining batter over the ripple mixture. Hold a knife upright in the pan and gently drag it through the batter several times to pull the ripple mixture throughout the cake.

8. Bake in the preheated oven for about 70 to 80 minutes or until a wooden skewer inserted into the center comes out clean.

9. Remove from the oven and allow to cool slightly in the pan then transfer to a wire rack to cool completely.

10. Meanwhile, prepare the orange glaze: Onto a large piece of parchment paper, sift the icing sugar. Transfer to a small bowl and whisk together with the orange juice until smooth and shiny.

11. Slowly pour the orange glaze over the top of the cake, and let it drizzle down the sides. Allow to the glaze to set for about 10 minutes before slicing.

To catch any drips when you are glazing the cake, place a cookie sheet under the wire rack. You can then move the cake to a cake stand or plate before serving for a clean finish.

I met our friends Brent and Nancy not long after Butter first opened. It is still the highlight of my week when they pop by on Saturday to visit and pick up some treats. Every week they select two treats each: one to eat on the spot (no bag required) and one to take home to enjoy on Sunday night while they're watching something fabulous on Masterpiece Theatre. As a general rule, we don't make angel food cake at Butter. But every year, on my dear friend Nancypants's birthday, I make an exception. Happy Birthday, Nancy!

Nancy's Birthday Cake

14 egg whites (see page 26)

2 teaspoons cream of tartar

¼ teaspoon salt

2 cups granulated sugar

1 ½ cups pastry flour

1 teaspoon pure vanilla

MAKES: 1 cake, about 8 to 10 slices

YOU WILL NEED: (9-inch) tube pan

1. Preheat the oven to 350°F.

2. In a stand mixer fitted with a whisk attachment, beat the egg whites on medium speed until foamy. Make sure your whisk attachment and bowl are wiped clean prior to beating the egg whites, as even a trace remnant of fat or oil will prevent them from becoming fluffy. Add the cream of tartar and salt. Turn the mixer to high and continue to beat until stiff peaks form.

3. Turn the mixer to medium and slowly beat in the sugar, a few tablespoons at a time. Turn the mixer to high and continue to beat until the egg whites are smooth and glossy, about 5 to 6 minutes.

4. Transfer the egg whites to a large bowl. Sift the flour over the egg whites and gently fold in with a spatula. Then fold in the vanilla.

5. Transfer the batter to the tube pan, then use a spatula to spread the batter evenly around the pan. Run a knife gently through the cake batter to release any air pockets.

6. Bake in the preheated oven for 40 to 45 minutes or until a wooden skewer inserted into the center comes out clean.

7. Remove from the oven. Invert the pan and place it over the neck of a wine bottle. (It sounds strange but, trust me, the cake won't fall out.) Allow to cool completely.

8. Remove the cake from the pan and turn it right side up to serve. You may need to run a small knife around the inside and outside edges of the pan to loosen the cake so it will drop.

You can serve this cake with berries and a big dollop of whipped cream, but for Nancy's birthday I always use a small offset spatula to ice it with our Marshmallow Fluff Frosting (page 137).

Cupcakes and Whoopie Pies

Chapter 7

*W*e are divided in my house over cupcakes. There are those of us who believe that a moist and delicious cupcake is really just a wonderful vehicle to get the butter cream to your mouth. Then there is Paul who enjoys his cupcakes naked (and by this I mean without butter cream on top, not that he likes to eat them in his birthday suit). India and I have tried to convince him to see the error of his ways. I have patiently explained to him that a cupcake without butter cream is simply a plain vanilla muffin. "What's wrong with that?" he asks. I guess when they're as fluffy and moist as these ones, it's pretty hard to argue with the guy.

Butter's Vanilla Cupcakes

2 cups pastry flour

1 cup all-purpose flour

2 teaspoons baking powder

½ teaspoon baking soda

½ teaspoon salt

1 cup butter, room temperature

2 cups granulated sugar

4 large eggs

1 cup buttermilk

1 teaspoon pure vanilla

FROSTING
Butter's Famous Butter Cream
(page 130)

MAKES: **18 cupcakes**

YOU WILL NEED: **2 muffin pans lined with paper liners, large ice cream scoop, small offset spatula or 14-inch piping bag fitted with a large star tip**

1. Preheat the oven to 350°F.

2. Onto a large piece of parchment paper, sift together both flours, baking powder, baking soda and salt. Set aside.

3. In a stand mixer fitted with a paddle attachment, cream the butter and sugar on medium to high speed until light and fluffy. Scrape down the sides of the bowl.

4. Add the eggs one at a time, and beat well after each addition. Scrape down the sides of the bowl several times.

5. In a liquid measuring cup, whisk together the milk and vanilla to combine.

6. Turn the mixer to low and add the dry ingredients in three parts, alternating with the liquid ingredients in two parts (begin and end with the dry). Scrape down the sides of the bowl several times to make sure everything is fully combined.

7. Use the ice cream scoop to fill each paper liner about three-quarters full with batter.

8. Bake in the preheated oven for 20 to 25 minutes or until a wooden skewer inserted into the center comes out clean.

9. Meanwhile, prepare your chosen flavor of Butter's Famous Butter Cream.

10. Remove the cupcakes from the oven and allow to cool in the pan for 10 minutes, then transfer to wire racks to cool completely.

11. Fill the piping bag with the butter cream of your choice and pipe the top of each cupcake (see Icing Cupcakes, page 143).

FROSTING

Some of our favorite frostings for Butter's Vanilla Cupcakes are:

- Vanilla (page 130)
- Hazelnut (page 131)
- Lemon (page 134)
- Cream Cheese (page 135)

The sky is the limit when it comes to finishing your cupcakes. We were feeling a little extravagant when we dusted this cupcake with white sprinkles and some mini white chocolate chips, then topped it with a blackberry jelly.

Here are some of our favorite
frostings for Butter's Chocolate
Cupcakes:

- Chocolate (page 133)
- Mint (page 131)
- Pistachio (page 131)
- Raspberry (page 131)
- Vanilla (page 130)

*N*othing could be more important for a chocolate cupcake than making sure it is moist and substantial. I tried lots of variations before I settled on this one. I guess I made the right choice because we get rave reviews on them every day!

Butter's Chocolate Cupcakes

2 ½ cups all-purpose flour

1 ¼ cups dark cocoa

1 ½ teaspoon baking soda

½ teaspoon salt

1 cup butter, room temperature

1 cup granulated sugar

1 cup dark brown sugar

3 large eggs

1 ½ cups whole milk

¾ cup sour cream

½ cup coffee, room temperature

2 teaspoons pure vanilla

FROSTING
Deep Dark Chocolate Butter Cream
    (page 133)

MAKES: 18 cupcakes

YOU WILL NEED: 2 muffin pans
    lined with paper liners, large
    ice cream scoop, small offset
    spatula or 14-inch piping bag
    fitted with a large star tip

1. Preheat the oven to 350°F.

2. Onto a large piece of parchment paper, sift together the flour, cocoa, baking soda and salt. Set aside.

3. In a stand mixer fitted with a paddle attachment, cream the butter and both sugars on medium to high speed until light and fluffy. Scrape down the sides of the bowl.

4. Add the eggs one at a time and beat well after each addition. Scrape down the sides of the bowl several times.

5. In a liquid measuring cup, whisk together the milk, sour cream, coffee and vanilla to combine.

6. Turn the mixer to low and add the dry ingredients in three parts, alternating with the liquid ingredients in two parts (begin and end with the dry). Scrape down the sides of the bowl several times.

7. Use the ice cream scoop to fill each paper liner about three-quarters full with batter.

8. Bake in the preheated oven for 20 to 25 minutes or until a wooden skewer inserted into the center comes out clean.

9. Meanwhile, prepare the Deep Dark Chocolate Butter Cream.

10. Remove the cupcakes from the oven and allow to cool in the pan for 10 minutes then transfer to wire racks to cool completely.

11. Fill the piping bag with the butter cream of your choice and pipe the top of each cupcake (see Icing Cupcakes, page 143).

Oh man, oh man! Just writing the name of this cupcake gets me excited! I really love butter cream, but boiled icing (or Marshmallow Fluff Frosting, as we call it) and I connect on a whole other level. I have been known to pop the tops off these cupcakes and gobble them down.

Chocolate Nutella High-Top Cupcakes

CUPCAKES

Butter's Chocolate Cupcakes (page 173)

FROSTING

Marshmallow Fluff Frosting (page 137)

Chocolate Glaze (page 137)

1 cup Nutella spread

18 hazelnuts

MAKES: 18 cupcakes

YOU WILL NEED: 2 muffin pans lined with paper liners, 14-inch piping bag fitted with a large round tip, small bowl (at least 4 inches deep)

BEFORE YOU BEGIN: Prepare a batch of Butter's Chocolate Cupcakes (page 173)

1. Place the cupcakes on a wire rack with a piece of parchment paper beneath it to catch any drips.

2. Use a paring knife to scoop out a piece of cake from the center of each cupcake, creating a well about 1 ½ inches across and 1 ½ inches deep. Fill each well with 1 teaspoon of Nutella.

> Don't hesitate to nibble on the little bits of cupcake you have scooped out—you will need energy to finish this project!

3. Prepare the Marshmallow Fluff Frosting. Fill the piping bag with the frosting and pipe the icing high on the top of each cupcake (see Icing Cupcakes, page 143) but no more than 3 inches high. The higher the frosting, the deeper the bowl you will need for the chocolate dip.

4. Prepare the Chocolate Glaze and transfer it to a small bowl (it should be at least 4 inches deep in the bowl).

5. Turn a frosted cupcake upside down and quickly dip it into the chocolate glaze. Coat all of the frosting in chocolate but do not touch the bottom of the bowl. (Move quickly—the frosting is sticky enough to hold onto the cupcake for a couple of seconds, but you run the risk of it falling off if you linger much longer.)

6. Return the cupcake to the wire rack and top with a hazelnut (to give people a little hint about the secret goodness hidden inside).

7. Repeat Steps 6 and 7 for each cupcake. Transfer the cupcakes to a platter and refrigerate to set the glaze, about 15 minutes.

Under normal circumstances I would tell you that you could use a small offset spatula to ice the cupcakes in lieu of a piping bag, but this cupcake really does require a piping bag for the finished "high-top" effect. If you don't have a piping bag or round tip, I suggest buying them—you'll want to make these cupcakes again and again!

When you were little, did your mom ever hide coins in your birthday cake? Mine didn't but my friend Lesley's mom did and I loved it. I am not sure if this was an early indication of my love of baked goods, or cash! I like to think it was the thrill of finding an unexpected surprise. With that in mind, I decided to stash a little peanut butter in the centers of these cupcakes. I find it goes down a little easier than a dime.

Chocolate Peanut Butter Crunch Cupcakes

2 ½ cups all-purpose flour

1 ¼ cups dark cocoa

1 ½ teaspoon baking soda

½ teaspoon salt

1 cup smooth peanut butter

½ cup butter, room temperature

1 cup granulated sugar

1 cup dark brown sugar

3 large eggs

1 ½ cups whole milk

1 cup sour cream

2 teaspoons pure vanilla

FROSTING

Peanut Butter Butter Cream
   (page 135)

Deep Dark Chocolate Butter Cream
   (page 133)

½ cup dark chocolate chips

½ cup Rice Krispies

MAKES: 18 cupcakes

YOU WILL NEED: 2 muffin pans lined
   with paper liners, large ice cream
   scoop, 2 (14-inch) piping bags,
   one fitted with a large round tip,
   one fitted with a large star tip

1. Preheat the oven to 350°F.

2. Onto a large piece of parchment paper, sift together the flour, cocoa, baking soda and salt. Set aside.

3. In a stand mixer fitted with a paddle attachment, cream ¹/₂ cup of the peanut butter with the butter and both sugars, on medium to high speed until light and fluffy. Scrape down the sides of the bowl.

If you prefer crunchy peanut butter, feel free to use it for the peanut butter center—but be sure to use smooth for the cupcake batter.

4. Add the eggs one at a time and beat well after each addition. Scrape down the sides of the bowl several times.

5. In a liquid measuring cup, whisk together the milk, sour cream and vanilla to combine.

6. Turn the mixer to low and add the dry ingredients in three parts, alternating with the liquid ingredients in two parts (begin and end with the dry). Scrape down the sides of the bowl several times to make sure everything is fully combined.

7. Use the ice cream scoop to fill each paper liner about three-quarters full with batter. Use two small teaspoons to push 1 teaspoon of peanut butter into the center of the batter and make sure it is fully covered by batter.

8. Bake in the preheated oven for 20 to 25 minutes or until a wooden skewer inserted into the side comes out clean.

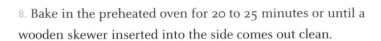

Don't put the skewer into the center of the cupcake because you will only hit peanut butter. When the cupcakes are nicely puffed up and the tops spring back when lightly pressed with a finger, you know they are ready.

9. Meanwhile, prepare the Peanut Butter Butter Cream and Deep Dark Chocolate Butter Cream.

10. Remove the cupcakes from the oven and allow to cool in the pan for 10 minutes, then transfer to wire racks to cool completely.

11. Fill the piping bag fitted with the large round tip with Peanut Butter Butter Cream and pipe one layer of icing on top of each cupcake (see Icing Cupcakes on page 143).

12. Fill the second piping bag with Chocolate Butter Cream and pipe a second layer of icing on top of the first, then sprinkle each cupcake with Rice Krispies.

13. In a small saucepan over low heat, melt the chocolate chips until smooth and shiny (or melt in the microwave for about 30 seconds on high). Use the back of a teaspoon to drizzle the chocolate on top of each cupcake.

BUTTER CREAM COMBINATIONS

Combining butter creams is a really fun way to create new cupcake variations. I love Peanut Butter Butter Cream (page 135) layered with Raspberry Butter Cream (page 131), and Cream Cheese Butter Cream (page 135) layered with Lemon Butter Cream (page 134). The possibilities and combinations are endless! Have some fun with it.

ho doesn't love fall? The smell of crisp September air, fallen leaves underfoot, new notebooks, freshly sharpened pencils and pumpkin. At Butter it is illegal to serve anything pumpkin before the new school year begins. Rules are rules. But come the first of September, the gloves are off and the smell of all things pumpkin fills the bakery.

Pumpkin Caramel Cupcakes

2 cups all-purpose flour

2 teaspoons baking powder

2 teaspoons cinnamon

1 teaspoon baking soda

1 teaspoon salt

1 teaspoon ground ginger

1 teaspoon nutmeg

1 cup vegetable oil

1 cup granulated sugar

1 cup dark brown sugar

4 large eggs

2 cups pumpkin puree

FROSTING
Cream Cheese Butter Cream
   (page 135)

Dulce de leche, for drizzling

MAKES: **18 cupcakes**

YOU WILL NEED: **2 muffin pans lined with paper liners, large ice cream scoop, small offset spatula or 14-inch piping bag fitted with a round tip**

1. Preheat the oven to 350°F.

2. In a large bowl, sift together the flour, baking powder, cinnamon, baking soda, salt, ground ginger and nutmeg. Set aside.

3. In another bowl, add the oil and both sugars and whisk to combine. Add the eggs one at a time and whisk after each addition.

4. Add the liquid ingredients to the dry ingredients and whisk until well combined. Add the pumpkin and whisk until fully combined.

5. Use the ice cream scoop to fill each paper liner about three-quarters full with batter.

6. Bake in the preheated oven for 20 to 25 minutes or until a wooden skewer inserted into the center comes out clean.

7. Meanwhile, prepare the Cream Cheese Butter Cream.

8. Remove the cupcakes from the oven and allow to cool in the pan for 10 minutes then transfer to wire racks to cool completely.

9. Fill the piping bag with the butter cream and pipe the top of each cupcake (see Icing Cupcakes, page 143). Use a teaspoon to drizzle a little dulce de leche on top of each cupcake for a lovely, tasty finish.

*M*y favorite part of my job at Butter is coming up with new and creative ways to put a spin on old standbys. I have always loved the graham cracker pie shell of a traditional lemon meringue pie. As a kid, I probably liked it more than the lemon and the meringue (though I did love eating all the little tips off the meringue, much to my mother's chagrin). In tribute to that memory I came up with this cupcake, and made some new and delicious memories along the way.

Ode to the Lemon Meringue Pie Cupcakes

½ cup Lemon Curd (page 205)

2 cups pastry flour

1 cup all-purpose flour

2 teaspoons baking powder

½ teaspoon baking soda

½ teaspoon salt

1 cup butter, room temperature

1 ½ cups granulated sugar

½ cup liquid honey

4 large eggs

1 cup whole milk

1 teaspoon pure vanilla

FROSTING
Marshmallow Fluff Frosting
(page 137)

MAKES: 18 cupcakes

YOU WILL NEED: 2 muffin pans lined with paper liners, large ice cream scoop, small offset spatula or 14-inch piping bag fitted with a large star tip, kitchen blowtorch (optional)

BEFORE YOU BEGIN: Prepare a batch of Lemon Curd (page 205)

1. Preheat the oven to 350°F.

2. Onto a large piece of parchment paper, sift together both flours, baking powder, baking soda and salt. Set aside.

3. In a stand mixer fitted with a paddle attachment, cream the butter, sugar and honey on medium to high speed until light and fluffy. Scrape down the sides of the bowl.

4. Add the eggs one at a time and beat well after each addition. Scrape down the sides of the bowl several times.

5. In a liquid measuring cup, whisk together the milk and vanilla to combine.

6. Turn the mixer to low and add the dry ingredients in three parts, alternating with the liquid ingredients in two parts (begin and end with the dry). Scrape down the sides of the bowl several times to make sure everything is fully combined.

7. Use the ice cream scoop to fill each paper liner about three-quarters full with batter.

8. Bake in the preheated oven for 20 to 22 minutes or until a wooden skewer inserted into the center comes out clean.

9. Remove the cupcakes from the oven and allow to cool in the pan for 10 minutes then transfer to wire racks to cool completely.

10. Use a paring knife to scoop out a piece of cake from the center of each cupcake, creating a well about 1 ½ inches across and 1 ½ inches deep (discard—or eat!—the piece of cupcake scooped out). Fill each well with 1 teaspoon of Lemon Curd.

11. Prepare the Marshmallow Fluff Frosting. Fill the piping bag with the frosting and pipe the top of each cupcake (see Icing Cupcakes, page 143).

If you have one on hand, use a kitchen blowtorch to gently brown the icing of each cupcake, as you would a lemon meringue pie (see page 203). Then sit down to enjoy a slice . . . er, I mean, a cupcake.

*P*eanut butter and jeeelllyyy . . . I like it when it's in my beeellllyyy! I'm not sure who wrote that little ditty, but they were bang on. This cupcake would also be amazing topped with Deep Dark Chocolate Butter Cream (page 133), but then we'd have to call it something else.

Peanut Butter and Jelly Cupcakes

2 cups pastry flour

1 cup all-purpose flour

2 teaspoons baking powder

½ teaspoon baking soda

½ teaspoon salt

¾ cup butter, room temperature

¼ cup smooth peanut butter

2 cups granulated sugar

4 large eggs

1 cup whole milk

1 teaspoon pure vanilla

½ cup raspberry jam

FROSTING

Peanut Butter Butter Cream
   (page 135)

½ cup honey roasted peanuts,
   chopped

MAKES: 18 cupcakes

YOU WILL NEED: 2 muffin pans
   lined with paper liners, large
   ice cream scoop, small offset
   spatula or 14-inch piping bag
   fitted with a large star tip

1. Preheat the oven to 350°F.

2. Onto a large piece of parchment paper, sift together both flours, baking powder, baking soda and salt. Set aside.

3. In a stand mixer fitted with a paddle attachment, cream the butter, peanut butter and sugar on medium to high speed until light and fluffy. Scrape down the sides of the bowl.

4. Add the eggs one at a time and beat well after each addition. Scrape down the sides of the bowl several times.

5. In a liquid measuring cup, whisk together the milk and vanilla to combine.

6. Turn the mixer to low and add the dry ingredients in three parts, alternating with the liquid ingredients in two parts (begin and end with the dry). Scrape down the sides of the bowl several times to make sure everything is fully combined.

7. Use the ice cream scoop to fill each paper liner about three-quarters full with batter.

8. Bake in the preheated oven for 20 to 25 minutes or until a wooden skewer inserted into the side comes out clean.

9. Meanwhile, prepare the Peanut Butter Butter Cream.

10. Remove the cupcakes from the oven and allow to cool in the pan for 10 minutes then transfer to wire racks to cool completely.

11. Use a paring knife to scoop out a piece of cake from the center of each cupcake, creating a well about $1\frac{1}{2}$ inches across and $1\frac{1}{2}$ inches deep (discard—or eat!—the piece of cupcake scooped out). Fill each well with 1 teaspoon of raspberry jam.

12. Fill the piping bag with the butter cream and pipe the top of each cupcake (see Icing Cupcakes, page 143). Sprinkle the top of each cupcake with chopped peanuts to finish.

*O*h, we were a happy bunch the day I came up with this. I never thought I would hear myself describing a cupcake as "refreshing," but I swear this one is. These are the perfect way to top off an alfresco dinner on a warm summer evening.

Lime White Chocolate Cupcake

2 cups pastry flour

1 cup all-purpose flour

2 teaspoons baking powder

½ teaspoon baking soda

½ teaspoon salt

1 cup butter, room temperature

2 cups granulated sugar

4 large eggs

¾ cup whole milk

¼ cup lime juice, freshly squeezed (about 2 limes)

Zest of 4 limes (reserve the zest of 1 for sprinkling)

1 teaspoon pure vanilla

LIME SYRUP

¼ cup lime juice, freshly squeezed (about 2 limes)

¼ cup granulated sugar

FROSTING

White Chocolate Butter Cream (page 134)

MAKES: 18 cupcakes

YOU WILL NEED: 2 muffin pans lined with paper liners, large ice cream scoop, small pastry brush, small offset spatula or 14-inch piping bag fitted with a large round tip

1. Preheat the oven to 350°F.

2. Onto a large piece of parchment paper, sift together both flours, baking powder, baking soda and salt. Set aside.

3. In a stand mixer fitted with a paddle attachment, cream the butter and sugar on medium to high speed until light and fluffy. Scrape down the sides of the bowl.

4. Add the eggs one at a time and beat well after each addition. Scrape down the sides of the bowl several times.

5. In a liquid measuring cup, whisk together the milk, lime juice, two-thirds of the lime zest and vanilla to combine.

6. Turn the mixer to low and add the dry ingredients in three parts, alternating with the liquid ingredients in two parts (begin and end with the dry). Scrape down the sides of the bowl several times to make sure everything is fully combined.

7. Use the ice cream scoop to fill each paper liner about three-quarters full with batter.

8. Bake in the preheated oven for 20 to 25 minutes or until a wooden skewer inserted into the center comes out clean.

9. Meanwhile, prepare the lime syrup: In a small saucepan over medium-high heat, bring the lime juice and sugar to a boil. Boil for 1 minute, then remove from the heat and allow to cool.

10. Remove the cupcakes from the oven. Use a wooden skewer to poke several holes in the top of each warm cupcake, then use the pastry brush to gently coat the top with syrup. Transfer to wire racks and cool completely.

11. Prepare the White Chocolate Butter Cream. Fill the piping bag with butter cream and pipe the top of each cupcake (see Icing Cupcakes, page 143). Sprinkle a little of the reserved lime zest on top of each cupcake for a pretty finish.

I like to believe that all things red velvet originated in the South, but there are endless stories about it originating at the Waldorf Astoria in New York. Apparently, a patron requested the recipe from the hotel staff and they obliged, but also included a bill for $350. In retaliation the guest circulated the recipe far and wide for free, to teach the hotel a lesson. That story doesn't paint the warm and homey image that this recipe deserves, so I'm going to stick with my Southern story, fantasy or not.

Red Velvet Cupcakes

2 cups pastry flour

½ cup all-purpose flour

2 tablespoons dark cocoa

2 teaspoons baking powder

½ teaspoon baking soda

½ teaspoon salt

2 cups granulated sugar

1 cup vegetable oil

1 cup buttermilk

4 large eggs

1 teaspoon white vinegar

1 teaspoon pure vanilla

1 tablespoon red food coloring

FROSTING
Cream Cheese Butter Cream
    (page 135)

1 cup walnuts, chopped

MAKES: 18 cupcakes

YOU WILL NEED: 2 muffin pans
    lined with paper liners, large ice
    cream scoop, 14-inch piping bag
    fitted with a large round tip

1. Preheat the oven to 350°F.

2. Onto a large piece of parchment paper, sift together both flours, cocoa, baking powder, baking soda and salt. Set aside.

3. In a large bowl, whisk together the sugar, oil, buttermilk, eggs, vinegar and vanilla until well combined. Add the red food coloring and whisk gently to combine. Sprinkle the dry ingredients over the liquid ingredients and whisk until just combined.

4. Use the ice cream scoop to fill each paper liner about three-quarters full with batter.

6. Bake in the preheated oven for 15 to 20 minutes or until a wooden skewer inserted into the center comes out clean.

7. Meanwhile, prepare the Cream Cheese Butter Cream.

8. Remove the cupcakes from the oven and cool in the pan for 10 minutes then transfer to wire racks to cool completely.

9. Fill the piping bag with frosting and pipe the top of each cupcake (see Icing Cupcakes, page 143). Sprinkle each cupcake with chopped walnuts to finish.

Be careful when whisking the batter—do it gently so as not to splash red dye all over the kitchen cupboards and youreslf!

I'm not really sure who came up with the idea for whoopie pie, but clearly the inventor was a culinary genius. I like to think of the whoopie pie as an inverted cupcake. They are more cake than cookie and, with the icing tucked in the middle, your fingers don't get too sticky. Genius I tell you, pure genius.

Red Velvet Whoopie Pies

1 cup butter

½ cup dark chocolate chips

2 ½ cups all-purpose flour

¼ cup dark cocoa

2 teaspoons baking powder

½ teaspoon baking soda

½ teaspoon salt

1 cup granulated sugar

¾ cup sour cream

2 large eggs

1 tablespoon white vinegar

1 teaspoon pure vanilla

1 tablespoon red food coloring

FROSTING
Cream Cheese Butter Cream
    (page 135)

MAKES: 10 whoopie pies

YOU WILL NEED: 2 cookie sheets
    lined with parchment paper,
    medium ice cream scoop, large
    piping bag fitted with a large
    round tip (optional)

1. Preheat the oven to 350°F.

2. In a small saucepan over low heat, melt the butter and chocolate (or melt in the microwave for about 30 seconds on high). Set aside to cool.

3. Onto a large piece of parchment paper, sift together the flour, cocoa, baking powder, baking soda and salt. Set aside.

4. In a large bowl, whisk together the sugar, sour cream, eggs, vinegar and vanilla to combine. Add the red food coloring and whisk gently. Add the melted chocolate and whisk to combine. Sprinkle the dry ingredients over the batter and whisk until well combined.

5. Use the ice cream scoop to drop the batter in 10 equal portions onto the prepared cookie sheets, about 1¹/₂ inches apart.

6. Bake in the preheated oven for 12 to 15 minutes or until the tops spring back when lightly pressed.

7. Meanwhile, prepare the Cream Cheese Butter Cream.

8. Remove the cookies from the oven and cool slightly on the cookie sheets, then transfer to wire racks to cool completely.

9. Turn half of the cookies bottom side up. Use the piping bag or two spoons to add a heaping tablespoon of butter cream onto each. Place the remaining cookies on top, right side up, and gently press to sandwich the two together.

The whoopie pies will keep in an airtight container for several days (but I'm pretty sure they will be gone within an hour).

If you don't have an ice cream scoop, you can use two large spoons, but the scoop really helps create a nice round whoopie pie shape.

Pastry, Pies and Tarts

Chapter 8

This is the pastry I grew up on, but in those days my mom made it with shortening. Given the name of my bakery, I felt the need to change the recipe up a little! You can easily double this recipe and keep half in the freezer—it's great to have the dough on hand for spur-of-the-moment pie cravings.

Butter's All Butter Pastry

5 cups all-purpose flour

1 teaspoon salt

2 cups butter, chilled and cut into
    1-inch cubes

1 large egg

1 tablespoon white vinegar

water

MAKES: enough for 4 (9-inch) single
    crust pies or 2 (9-inch) double
    crust pies

YOU WILL NEED: (9-inch) pie dish
    per pie, pastry cutter

This dough is best made the day before you need it so it can chill overnight. You can store the dough wrapped tightly in plastic wrap in the refrigerator for up to 3 days or in the freezer for up to 1 month.

PREPARING THE DOUGH

1. Place the flour and salt in a large bowl. Scatter the butter over the flour mixture. Use the pastry cutter to cut the butter into the flour until the mixture forms large pea-sized crumbs (see page 25). You should still be able to recognize some of the butter.

2. Crack the egg into a liquid measuring cup and add the vinegar. Top with enough cold water to reach a 1-cup measure. Whisk until combined, then pour over the flour mixture.

3. Mix with a fork until the dough starts to pull together. Gently use your hands to finish mixing the dough until it comes together enough to shape. You should still see some butter bits throughout.

4. Shape the dough into four evenly sized disks about $1/2$ inch thick each and wrap separately in plastic wrap. Refrigerate for at least 2 hours or overnight.

ROLLING THE DOUGH

Lightly dust a work surface with flour and place a chilled disk of dough in the center of it. The kitchen countertop will work just fine for rolling, but if you have space for a piece of marble (a 24- × 24-inch piece is ideal), your pastry will thank you. The marble's cool surface will keep the pastry cool.

Use a rolling pin to roll from the center of the dough out toward the edges, rotating every few strokes to make sure it doesn't stick. Lightly dust the work surface with more flour as needed. Treat your rolling pin like an extension of your arms—don't be afraid of it!

Be careful not to overwork the dough so that all the butter chunks disappear. You want to be able to see the butter chunks as these are the key to achieving a light, flaky pastry. Every time a piece of dough is rolled it warms up and the butter chunks inside it soften and become more incorporated. This makes the butter less likely to melt and steam during baking, resulting in pastry that is tough and dense, rather than flaky and light. If the dough gets too warm when you are rolling it, place it back in the refrigerator for a few minutes until it has chilled again.

I don't believe in rolling dough more than once. I think it's better to work with as much as you need and keep the rest in the refrigerator, rather than rolling out a huge piece and trimming away lots of excess. If you need to reroll dough trimmings, chill them in the refrigerator first.

MAKING A SINGLE CRUST PIE

1. Use a rolling pin to roll one chilled disk of dough out to about ⅛ inch thick (about 11 inches in diameter, 2 inches larger than pie dish). Carefully fold into quarters and gently transfer to the pie dish. Unfold and press into place lightly.

2. Trim the dough with a knife, kitchen scissors or a metal bench scraper to leave about a 1-inch overhang over the edge of the dish. The best way to judge this is to trim the pastry at the point where it just touches the work surface. Roll and tuck the 1-inch overhang back under the edge of the pie shell.

> You can either finish here and leave the edge plain, or you can pinch it into pleasing points as we do at the bakery (follow Step 3 below).

3. Use your index finger to push finger-sized sections of dough from the inside edge of the pie, out and over the edge of the pie dish. Use the index finger and thumb on your opposite hand to pinch each section into a point. Continue this process all around the edge of the pie shell until you end up where you began and, voilà, pleasing points!

MAKING A DOUBLE CRUST PIE

1. Use a rolling pin to roll one chilled disk of dough out to about ⅛ inch thick (about 11 inches in diameter, 2 inches larger than pie dish). Carefully fold into quarters and gently transfer to the pie dish. Unfold and press into place lightly.

2. Trim the dough with a knife, kitchen scissors or metal bench scraper to leave about a ½-inch overhang over the edge of the dish.

3. Fill the pie with your chosen filling and dot with chilled butter as directed.

4. Repeat Step 1 with a second disk of dough and unfold on top of the pie filling, leaving about a 1-inch overhang over the edge of the dish.

5. Roll and tuck the dough edge back under the bottom edge of the pie shell. Seal the pie by pressing the tines of a fork all around the edge of the pie shell to create a simple, uniform pattern. Alternatively, finish it in pleasing points (follow Step 3 of making a single crust pie).

1. Use a rolling pin to roll one chilled disk of dough out to about ⅛ inch thick (about 11 inches in diameter, 2 inches larger than pie dish). Carefully fold into quarters and gently transfer to the pie dish. Unfold and lightly press into place.

2. Trim the dough with a knife, kitchen scissors or metal bench scraper to leave about a 1-inch overhang over the edge of the dish.

3. Fill the pie with your chosen filling and dot with chilled butter as directed.

4. Use a rolling pin to roll out a second disk of dough, this time to about 3 inches larger than the pie dish, and cut the dough into twelve 1-inch-wide strips.

5. Start at one edge of the pie and lay half the strips very carefully across it, vertically, about ½ inch apart. Allow the extra length of each strip to hang over the edges of the dish.

6. Fold every second strip of dough back in half on top of itself, toward the opposite edge of the pie. Place a new strip of dough horizontally across the center of the pie on top of the remaining strips. Allow the extra length of the strip to hang over the edges of the dish. Unfold the folded strips back over the horizontal strip.

7. Fold the alternating strips of dough (those that haven't been moved yet) back toward the opposite edge of the pie. Place a second horizontal strip across the pie, about ½ inch apart from the first. Unfold the folded strips back over this horizontal strip, and you will begin to see the lattice pattern forming.

8. Repeat this process, weaving the strips of dough, until the one half of the pie is complete. Then turn the dish around and repeat the process on the other half of the pie.

9. Trim the overhanging strips of dough with a knife, kitchen scissors or metal bench scraper to leave a 1-inch overhang over the edge of the pie dish.

10. Roll and tuck the overhanging edges back under the bottom pie shell. Seal the edges by pressing the tines of a fork all around the edge of the pie shell to create a simple, uniform pattern. Alternatively, finish it with pleasing points (follow Step 3 of making a single crust pie on page 194).

*T*his is a wonderful cookie-like pastry that is easy to make, easy to handle and bakes up perfectly every time. You can freeze the baked tart shells to have them ready to be filled for emergency dessert situations.

Short but Sweet Pastry

1 ½ cups butter, room temperature

1 cup granulated sugar

2 large eggs

4 cups all-purpose flour

½ teaspoon salt

MAKES: 2 (9-inch) tart shells

YOU WILL NEED: 2 (9-inch) tart pans, pastry docker (or fork if you do not have one)

Carefully wrapped in plastic wrap, the tart shells will store in the freezer for up to 2 months.

1. Preheat the oven to 350°F.

2. In a stand mixer fitted with a paddle attachment, cream the butter and sugar on medium to high speed until light and fluffy. Scrape down the sides of the bowl.

3. Add the eggs one at a time and beat after each addition. Scrape down the sides of the bowl.

4. Turn the mixer to low and slowly add the flour and salt until fully combined. Turn the mixer to high and mix until the dough pulls from the sides of the bowl and comes together.

5. Shape the dough into two equally sized disks about ¹/₂ inch thick each and wrap separately in plastic wrap. Refrigerate for at least 2 hours or overnight.

6. Use a rolling pin to roll one chilled disk of dough out to about ¹/₄ inch thick (for tips on rolling dough see page 193). Carefully fold into quarters and gently transfer to the tart pan. Unfold and press into place lightly.

7. Roll the rolling pin across the top of the tart pan to trim the top edge of the tart shell and give a clean edge. Roll the pastry docker over the bottom of the shell to prevent air bubbles forming when baking.

8. Repeat Steps 6 and 7 with the second disk of dough.

9. Bake in the preheated oven for 25 minutes or until the tart shells are a light golden brown.

10. Remove from the oven and allow to cool slightly in the pans then transfer to wire racks to cool completely.

*O*f all the reasons that exist for being a proud Canadian, getting to take credit for coming up with the butter tart is one of my favorites. There are a lot of variations out there, but I think this one, my mom's own recipe, is the best by far.

The Quintessential Butter Tart

1 Butter's All Butter Pastry
    (page 192)

3 large eggs

1 ½ cups light brown sugar

1 ½ teaspoons pure vanilla

¾ teaspoon lemon juice

½ teaspoon salt

3 cups sultana raisins

MAKES: **24 tarts**

YOU WILL NEED: **5-inch circular cutter, 2 muffin pans**

BEFORE YOU BEGIN: **Prepare Butter's All Butter Pastry recipe, up to the end of Step 4 (page 192)**

1. Preheat the oven to 350°F.

2. Use a rolling pin to roll out one disk of chilled dough to about ¹/₈ inch thick (for tips on rolling dough see page 193). Use the circular cutter to cut out 24 circles.

2. Take each circle and pinch it at two points, best visualized as 3 o'clock and 9 o'clock. Pinch it again at 12 o'clock and 6 o'clock as you lift and place it into the muffin cup. This gives a four-leaf clover shape to the shell. Refrigerate until ready to be filled.

4. In a medium bowl, whisk together the eggs, sugar, vanilla, lemon juice and salt until well combined. Transfer the egg and sugar mixture to a liquid measuring cup with a spout.

5. Remove the muffin pans from the refrigerator and fill each tart shell with about 2 tablespoons of raisins. Then top with the egg and sugar mixture until two-thirds full.

> Try not to spill the filling down the sides of the shells, as this can cause a huge problem when removing the baked butter tarts from the pan.

6. Bake in the preheated oven for 20 to 25 minutes or until the pastry is nicely browned and the centers of the tarts are puffed and golden.

7. Remove from the oven and allow to cool slightly in the pan then transfer to wire racks to cool completely. You may need to use a small knife to help lift the tarts from the cups.

These butter tarts will keep in an airtight container for 1 week or in the freezer for up to 1 month.

This tart is super-easy to make but still so elegant in its simplicity. Whether you choose to make one large tart or more personal-sized ones, you can mix up the nut combinations any way you like. Or you can be a purist and just stick with one kind of nut. Either way, they are delicious served with a big dollop of whipped cream on top.

Oh, You Nutty Tart!

1 (9-inch) or 8 (3-inch) Short but Sweet Pastry tart shells (page 197), prebaked

1 cup walnuts, chopped

½ cup pecans, chopped

½ cup hazelnuts, chopped

⅔ cup dark brown sugar

¼ cup butter

¼ cup dark corn syrup

2 tablespoons heavy cream

MAKES: 1 tart, about 8 to 10 slices, or 8 individual little tarts

YOU WILL NEED: (9-inch) tart pan or 8 (3-inch) tart pans, cookie sheet

BEFORE YOU BEGIN: Prebake a Short but Sweet Pastry tart shell (page 197) or 8 little tart shells (see note below)

1. Preheat the oven to 375°F.

2. Place the nuts on a cookie sheet and bake in the preheated oven for about 5 to 7 minutes or until lightly toasted. Flip the nuts with a metal spatula halfway to ensure even toasting. Remove from the oven and set aside to cool.

3. In a medium saucepan over medium heat, combine the sugar, butter, corn syrup and cream. Stir constantly and bring to a boil. Allow to boil for 1 minute.

4. Sprinkle the nuts into the prepared tart shell(s). Pour the hot syrup evenly over them.

5. Bake in the preheated oven for 10 to 12 minutes or until the tart mixture is bubbling.

6. Remove from the oven and allow to cool on a wire rack.

To make these tarts little you will need 8 (3-inch) tart pans and a 4-inch circular cutter. Use the cutter to cut out 8 circles of dough at Step 6 of the Short but Sweet Pastry recipe, then gently lift and place each disk of dough into its own individual pan before continuing with the recipe.

One day a few years back, we had a couple visit us at the bakery who claimed that they make a point of tasting lemon tarts wherever they travel. Having traveled the world far and wide, they both agreed that Butter's version was the best they had ever had. They even went so far as to claim it was better than those they had tasted by some pretty famous bakers. I'm not sure if that really is the case, but it sure was nice to hear. It reminded me how important it is to share a compliment with someone for a job well done.

Butter's Lemon Meringue Tart

1 (9-inch) Short but Sweet Pastry
    tart shell (page 197), prebaked

Lemon Curd (page 205)

4 egg whites (see page 26)

1 cup granulated sugar

MAKES: **1 pie, about 8 to 10 slices**

YOU WILL NEED: **(9-inch) tart pan,
kitchen blowtorch**

BEFORE YOU BEGIN: **Prebake a Short but Sweet Pastry tart shell (page 197) and prepare a batch of Lemon Curd (page 205)**

1. Fill the prebaked tart shell with enough Lemon Curd that it reaches the top edge. Use a small offset spatula to smooth it across the top. Refrigerate until ready to be topped with the meringue.

2. In a stand mixer fitted with a whisk attachment add the egg whites (make sure the bowl is very clean first) and then the sugar and whisk to combine.

3. Bring a small saucepan of water to a boil and rest the bowl of the stand mixer over the top of it, but do not let the bottom of the bowl touch the water. Heat the egg whites and whisk to dissolve the sugar. To test for doneness, rub the heated egg and sugar mixture between your fingers—when you can no longer feel any grain they are ready to remove from the heat.

You could use a double boiler here, but I find it much more efficient to use the bowl of the stand mixer instead of transferring the egg mixture from bowl to bowl.

5. Return the bowl to the stand mixer. Whip the egg white mixture on high speed until stiff peaks form but the mixture is still shiny and smooth, between 5 and 7 minutes.

Take care not to overwhip the meringue mixture. If you do, the egg whites will appear to separate and lose their smooth silky look, and it will be difficult to spread the meringue on the tart.

6. Remove the filled tart shell from the refrigerator and gently drop large spoonfuls of the meringue on top of the lemon curd. Use a small offset spatula or knife to spread the meringue to the edge of the tart shell. Lift the meringue with the edge of the spatula or knife to create pointed peaks—the higher the better!

7. Use a kitchen blowtorch to slowly and carefully brown the top of the tart. Hold the blowtorch at least 3 inches from the top of the tart and keep it moving back and forth. If you hold the torch too close or for too long in one spot, you run the risk of burning the tips.

This tart is best served the day you make it, but it will keep in the refrigerator for a few days more.

I've come to discover that a really delicious lemon curd is one of life's little necessities. There are so many wonderful ways it can be used to create simple yet delicious desserts. It serves as the base to Butter's Lemon Meringue Tart (page 203), which we top with a lovely, silky meringue. But you can just as easily fold some whipped cream into the curd and spoon it over angel food cake, served with berries. Even a large spoonful on top of some plain yogurt with granola is a nice way to start your day.

Lemon Curd

1 cup lemon juice, freshly squeezed
    (about 4 lemons)

6 large eggs

1 cup granulated sugar

½ teaspoon salt

1 cup butter, chilled and cut into
    1-inch cubes

MAKES: **3 cups, enough for
    1 (9-inch) tart or pie**

YOU WILL NEED: **candy thermom-
    eter, blender**

1. In a medium saucepan over medium heat, whisk together the lemon juice, eggs, sugar and salt. Measure the temperature with the candy thermometer and whisk until it reaches 180°F. The eggs should be quite thick and pale in color. Remove from the heat and allow to cool for a few moments.

2. Carefully pour the hot curd into the blender and securely affix the lid. Blend on medium to high speed and add the butter piece by piece. Make sure each piece is fully incorporated before adding the next. Once all the butter is incorporated, the curd should be thick and creamy.

3. Use a sieve to strain the curd into a glass or ceramic mixing bowl. The curd will be quite thick at this point, but still too loose to use.

4. Place a piece of plastic wrap directly on top of the curd and refrigerate overnight. Once set, the curd should be thick enough to spread with a knife.

This curd can be kept in the refrigerator, in a covered bowl or an airtight container, for up to 1 week.

Have you ever wished that you could capture the sense of freedom you felt as a child as the end of the school year approached and the summer months stretched out ahead? Hot days playing in the sprinkler and long, warm evenings to run with your friends until sundown. In a bite this pie brings it all back for me. Make sure you are eating it on the front porch, barefoot after a long game of kick the can.

Strawberry Rhubarb Almond Pie

1 Butter's All Butter Pastry double crust pie (page 192)

1 ¼ cups granulated sugar

¼ cup ground almonds

2 large egg yolks

2 cups strawberries, stems removed, washed, dried and halved

2 cups rhubarb, cut into 1-inch pieces (fresh or frozen)

3 tablespoons cornstarch

2 tablespoons instant tapioca

½ teaspoon salt

3 tablespoons butter, chilled and cut into 6 pieces

FINISHING

1 large egg

2 tablespoon cold water

Coarse sanding sugar, for sprinkling

MAKES: 1 pie, about 8 to 10 slices

YOU WILL NEED: (9-inch) pie dish

BEFORE YOU BEGIN: Prepare Butter's All Butter Pastry (page 192) and follow the steps for making a double crust pie (page 194)

1. Preheat the oven to 350°F.

2. In a small bowl, combine ¼ cup of the sugar, the ground almonds and egg yolks. Stir to create a smooth paste. Spread evenly on the bottom of the prepared pie shell.

3. In a large bowl, combine the strawberries, rhubarb, cornstarch, tapioca, salt and remaining 1 cup of sugar. Gently stir to evenly coat the fruit.

4. Pour the fruit filling on top of the almond filling and dot with the chilled butter.

At this point, you can either top the pie with a second pastry crust and make a double crust pie, or you can create a lattice-top pie as shown in the photo (follow the steps for both on pages 194 and 196). If you opt for the double crust pie, cut several slits about 2 inches in length across the top of the pie to allow the steam and juices to escape.

5. In a small bowl, whisk together the egg and water to create an egg wash. Use a pastry brush to gently coat the top of the pie with the wash. Sprinkle with a little sanding sugar.

6. Bake in the preheated oven for 50 to 60 minutes or until the juice from the fruit is bubbling and the pastry is golden brown.

7. Remove from the oven and allow to cool on a wire rack for at least 2 to 3 hours to allow the juices to set before slicing.

This recipe came to me from my dear friend Margie. We became fast friends the day our family moved onto the block. You couldn't ask for a better neighbor, and when I found out she was a keen baker I knew she was one for keeps! I think this may be my all-time favorite pie. The combination of sour cream, rhubarb and crumb topping is so good, it should be illegal.

Sour Cream Rhubarb Pie

1 Butter's All Butter Pastry single crust pie (page 192)

1 ¼ cups sugar

3 tablespoons all-purpose flour

½ teaspoon salt

2 large eggs

1 cup sour cream

1 teaspoon pure vanilla

3 cups rhubarb (fresh or frozen), cut into ½-inch pieces

CRUMB TOPPING

⅓ cup sugar

⅓ cup all-purpose flour

¼ teaspoon salt

1 teaspoon cinnamon

¼ cup butter, softened

MAKES: 1 pie, about 8 to 10 slices

YOU WILL NEED: (9-inch) pie dish

BEFORE YOU BEGIN: Prepare Butter's All Butter Pastry (page 192) and follow the steps for making a single crust pie (page 194)

1. Preheat the oven to 400°F.

2. In a large bowl, combine the sugar, flour and salt. In a separate bowl, whisk together the eggs, sour cream and vanilla, then add to the flour mixture.

3. Place the rhubarb in the prepared pie shell. Pour the egg and flour mixture evenly over the top.

4. Bake in the preheated oven for 10 minutes. Lower the oven temperature to 350°F and bake for 30 minutes more.

5. Meanwhile, in a small bowl, combine the ingredients for the crumb topping and mix with a fork until crumbly.

6. Remove the pie from the oven and sprinkle the crumb topping over the top. Return to the oven to bake for another 15 minutes or until the topping is lightly browned.

7. Remove from the oven again and allow the pie to cool slightly before slicing.

Margie has frozen this baked pie. She tells me that once it is defrosted and warmed slightly in a 200°F oven, you would never know it had ever been frozen.

*O*h, this is a good one! It couldn't be easier to make, and while I love this pie the day it is made, I love it even more, thinly sliced, right out of the refrigerator the morning after. Let's keep that our little secret, okay?

Chocolate Chip Walnut Pie

1 Butter's All Butter Pastry single crust pie (page 192)

1 cup butter

2 large eggs

1 cup dark brown sugar

1 teaspoon pure vanilla

½ cup all-purpose flour

½ teaspoon salt

1 cup dark chocolate chips

1 cup walnuts, chopped

MAKES: **1 pie, about 8 to 10 slices**

YOU WILL NEED: **(9-inch) pie dish**

BEFORE YOU BEGIN: **Prepare Butter's All Butter Pastry (page 192) and follow the steps for making a single crust pie (page 194)**

1. Preheat the oven to 350°F.

2. In a small saucepan over low heat, melt the butter. Set aside to cool.

3. In a large bowl, whisk the eggs, sugar and vanilla until fully combined. Add the flour and salt and whisk until well combined. Then whisk in the melted butter slowly, so as not to splash it out of the bowl.

4. Sprinkle the chocolate chips and walnuts into the prepared pie shell. Pour the filling evenly over the top.

5. Bake in the preheated oven for 45 to 55 minutes or until the filling is puffed and golden brown.

6. Remove from the oven and allow the pie to cool on a wire rack before slicing.

My best friend, Jan, has three boys and her youngest, Ayden, is addicted to my bumbleberry pie. From quite a young age he has been able to finish a whole pie with little effort. I can't imagine a bigger compliment. I cannot think of this pie without thinking of Ayden.

Bumbleberry Pie for Ayden

1 Butter's All Butter Pastry double crust pie (page 192)

1 cup blueberries

1 cup strawberries, stems removed and quartered

1 cup blackberries

1 cup raspberries

1 cup granulated sugar

3 tablespoons cornstarch

2 tablespoons instant tapioca

½ teaspoon salt

3 tablespoons butter, chilled and cut into 6 pieces

FINISHING

1 large egg

2 tablespoons cold water

Coarse sanding sugar, for sprinkling

MAKES: 1 pie, about 8 to 10 slices (or 1 if you are like Ayden)

YOU WILL NEED: (9-inch) pie dish

BEFORE YOU BEGIN: Prepare Butter's All Butter Pastry (page 192) and follow the steps for making a double crust pie (page 194)

1. Preheat the oven to 350°F.

2. In a large bowl, combine the berries, sugar, cornstarch, tapioca and salt. Gently stir to evenly coat the fruit.

3. Fill the prepared pie shell with the fruit and dot with the chilled butter. Follow the steps on page 194 to top the pie with a second pastry shell to make a double crust pie. Cut several slits about 2 inches in length in the top of the pie to allow the steam and juices to escape.

4. In a small bowl, whisk together the egg and water to make an egg wash. Use a pastry brush to gently coat the top of the pie with the wash. Sprinkle with a little sanding sugar.

5. Bake in the preheated oven for 50 to 60 minutes or until the juice from the fruit is bubbling up and the pastry is golden brown.

6. Remove from the oven and allow to cool on a wire rack for at least 2 to 3 hours to allow the juices to set before slicing.

If fresh fruit is not available, frozen berries work just fine.

I have never been a coffee drinker—I just don't like the taste. Perhaps if a cup of joe tasted like this pie I could be convinced to change my ways.

Chocolate Espresso Pecan Pie

1 Butter's All Butter Pastry single crust pie (page 192)

⅓ cup dark chocolate chips

2 tablespoons butter

1 tablespoon instant espresso powder

1 tablespoon hot water

2 large eggs

½ cup dark brown sugar

½ cup clear corn syrup

½ teaspoon salt

1 tablespoon bourbon

1 ¼ cups whole pecans

MAKES: 1 pie, about 8 to 10 slices

YOU WILL NEED: (9-inch) pie dish

BEFORE YOU BEGIN: Prepare Butter's All Butter Pastry (page 192) and follow the steps for making a single crust pie (page 194)

1. Preheat the oven to 350°F.

2. In a small saucepan over medium heat, combine the chocolate chips and butter and melt until smooth.

3. In a small bowl, dissolve the espresso powder in the hot water.

4. In a large bowl, whisk together the eggs, sugar, corn syrup, melted chocolate and salt. Add the espresso and bourbon and whisk to incorporate.

5. Fill the prepared pie shell with the pecans. Pour the chocolate-espresso filling over the top. Shake the pie a little to level the filling.

6. Bake in the preheated oven for 45 to 50 minutes or until the filling has puffed up and is starting to crack.

7. Remove from the oven and allow to cool on a wire rack for at least 3 hours, or overnight, so the filling has set and will cut cleanly when slicing.

his is another of Paul's favorites. It couldn't be simpler to prepare and is a lovely choice in early summer when raspberries are abundant. Blueberries or blackberries are yummy alternatives.

Raspberry Custard Pie

1 Butter's All Butter Pastry single crust pie (page 192)

2 cups fresh raspberries

¾ cup plus 2 tablespoons granulated sugar

2 tablespoons all-purpose flour

1 cup heavy cream

2 large eggs

¼ teaspoon salt

MAKES: **1 pie, about 8 to 10 slices**

YOU WILL NEED: **(9-inch) pie dish**

BEFORE YOU BEGIN: **Prepare Butter's All Butter Pastry (page 192) and follow the steps for making a single crust pie (page 194)**

1. Preheat the oven to 375°F.

2. Place the raspberries in a small bowl and sprinkle 2 tablespoons of the sugar over the top. Stir very gently to combine to avoid crushing the raspberries.

3. In large bowl, whisk together the remaining ¾ cup of sugar, flour, cream, eggs and salt to make the custard.

4. Carefully pour the custard into the prepared pie shell. Gently sprinkle the raspberries evenly throughout the custard.

5. Bake in the preheated oven for 45 to 50 minutes or until the custard has set and is very lightly browned.

6. Remove from the oven and allow to cool completely on a wire rack before slicing.

or me, apple pie is all about the fall. It is not a pie to be served in the heat of summer, but rather on a chilly October evening after a big bowl of veal stew. I like to top it with a wedge of old cheddar or a scoop of vanilla ice cream. I also think it tastes better when eaten curled up on the sofa in front of a roaring fire, but I'm a stickler for details.

Good Ol' Apple Pie

1 Butter's All Butter Pastry double crust pie (page 192)

7 to 8 apples (I like to use a mix of Granny Smith and Ambrosia)

Lemon juice, about 1 teaspoon

½ cup dark brown sugar

2 tablespoons all-purpose flour

2 tablespoons cornstarch

1 teaspoon cinnamon

1 teaspoon pure vanilla

3 tablespoons butter, chilled and cut into 6 pieces

FINISHING

1 large egg

2 tablespoons cold water

Coarse sanding sugar, for sprinkling

MAKES: **1 pie, about 8 to 10 slices**

YOU WILL NEED: **(9-inch) pie dish**

BEFORE YOU BEGIN: **Prepare Butter's All Butter Pastry (page 192) and follow the steps for making a double crust pie (page 194)**

1. Preheat the oven to 350°F.

2. Wash the apples with cool water and peel them with a vegetable peeler or paring knife. Quarter each apple, trim off the core and cut each quarter into four slices. As you slice the apples, place them in a large bowl that has a squeeze of lemon juice in it. Use a large spoon to gently toss the apples in the juice to help prevent the apples from browning.

3. Add the sugar, flour, cornstarch, cinnamon and vanilla to the apples. Gently stir with a large spoon to evenly coat the fruit.

4. Spoon the apples evenly into the prepared pie shell. Dot with the chilled butter. Follow the steps on page 194 to top the pie with a second pastry shell and make a double crust pie. Cut several slits about 2 inches in length in the top of the pie to allow the steam and juices to escape.

If you are feeling confident, you can also use a paring knife to cut a very basic outline of an apple with stem and leaf into the center of the top pie crust.

5. In a small bowl, whisk together the egg and water to make an egg wash. Use a pastry brush to gently coat the top of the pie with the wash. Sprinkle with a little sanding sugar.

6. Bake in the preheated oven for 50 to 60 minutes or until the juice from the fruit is bubbling up through the top of the pie and the pastry is golden brown.

7. Remove from the oven and allow to cool on a wire rack for at least 2 hours, to allow the juices in the pie to set before slicing.

*T*he first time I set out to create pumpkin pie at Butter was in the wee hours of a September morning, with Thanksgiving fast approaching. Traditionally, pumpkin pie calls for evaporated milk, but I was tired and not thinking straight and I grabbed the condensed milk. I should bake half-asleep more often because that little error created the most delicious pie.

The Only Pumpkin Pie

1 Butter's All Butter Pastry single crust pie (page 192)

2 large eggs

2 cups pumpkin puree

1 ½ cups granulated sugar

1 teaspoon cinnamon

½ teaspoon salt

½ teaspoon ground ginger

¼ teaspoon ground cloves

¼ teaspoon nutmeg

1 300-mL can condensed milk (about 1 ¼ cups)

MAKES: **1 pie, about 8 to 10 slices**

YOU WILL NEED: **(9-inch) pie dish**

BEFORE YOU BEGIN: **Prepare Butter's All Butter Pastry (page 192) and follow the steps for making a single crust pie (page 194)**

1. Preheat the oven to 375°F.

2. In a large bowl, whisk the eggs, pumpkin puree, sugar, cinnamon, salt, ground ginger, cloves, nutmeg and condensed milk until fully combined.

3. Pour the pumpkin filling into the prepared pie shell.

4. Bake in the preheated oven for 40 to 45 minutes or until the edges of the filling have set and the center is just barely loose (a knife inserted halfway between the edge of the pie and the center should come out clean) and the pastry is golden brown.

5. Remove from the oven and allow to cool on a wire rack before slicing. Serve with a good dollop of whipped cream.

You can prepare the filling as much as a day in advance and keep it in the refrigerator until you are ready to bake this pie.

*W*hat the heck is Shoo Fly Pie, you ask? It is a funny, strange and truly yummy combination of pie, cake and molasses. You may be a little confused when assembling this pie because it doesn't appear that it should work, but stick with it for a lovely surprise ending.

Shoo Fly Pie

1 Butter's All Butter Pastry single crust pie (page 192)

½ cup fancy molasses

1 teaspoon baking soda

1 cup boiling water

1 ½ cups all-purpose flour

1 cup dark brown sugar

½ teaspoon cinnamon

¾ cup butter, chilled

MAKES: **1 pie, about 8 to 10 slices**

YOU WILL NEED: **(9-inch) pie dish, pastry cutter**

BEFORE YOU BEGIN: **Prepare Butter's All Butter Pastry (page 192) and follow the steps for making a single crust pie (page 194)**

1. Preheat the oven to 350°F.

2. In a small bowl, combine the molasses and baking soda. Carefully whisk in the boiling water.

3. In another bowl, combine the flour, sugar and cinnamon. Use a pastry cutter to cut in the chilled butter until crumbly.

4. Pour one-third of the molasses mixture into the prepared pie shell and top with one-third of the flour and butter mixture. Repeat this process twice more, finishing with the flour mixture.

5. Bake in the preheated oven for 40 to 45 minutes or until the center has puffed up and the pastry is golden brown.

6. Remove from the oven and allow to cool on a wire rack before serving.

Confections

Chapter 9

*I*f there is one item that really put Butter on the map, I would have to say it's our marshmallows. Back in 2007, when Butter first opened, the gourmet marshmallow was still a bit of a mystery. Most people didn't know there was a tasty alternative to store-bought marshmallows available. But word soon got out, people started talking, and my brain got ticking. Butter now makes 18 flavors of marshmallows, and I'm always coming up with new varieties—but Butter's Vanilla Marshmallows are the classic we opened our doors with.

Butter's Famous Marshmallows

1 cup water

3 envelopes unflavored gelatin

2 cups granulated sugar

½ cup light corn syrup

½ teaspoon salt

2 tablespoons pure vanilla

Generous amount of icing sugar to coat the marshmallows, about 2 cups

MAKES: About 64 (1- × 1-inch) marshmallows

YOU WILL NEED: (9- × 9-inch) baking pan, buttered

1. In a stand mixer fitted with a whisk attachment, pour in ½ cup of the water and sprinkle with the gelatin. Set aside to allow the gelatin to soak in.

2. In a medium saucepan over high heat, add the sugar, corn syrup, salt and remaining ½ cup of water. Bring to a rolling boil and continue to boil for 1 minute. Remove from the heat.

3. Turn the mixer to low and mix the gelatin once or twice to combine it with the water. Slowly add the hot sugar mixture, pouring it gently down the side of the bowl, and continue to mix on low.

Be really careful at this point because the sugar mixture is smoking hot! It's not a job for little ones.

4. Turn the mixer to high and continue to whip for 10 to 12 minutes until the marshmallow batter almost triples in size and becomes very thick. Scrape down the sides of the bowl frequently to avoid the batter overflowing as it grows. Stop the mixer, add the vanilla, and then whip briefly to combine.

5. Transfer the mixture to the prepared baking pan and use a spatula or bench scraper to spread it evenly in the pan. Work quickly, as the marshmallow becomes more difficult to manipulate as it sets.

6. Grease a sheet of plastic wrap with butter and lay it across the top of the marshmallow. Press down firmly on the plastic wrap, to seal it smoothly and tightly against the mixture.

7. Leave the marshmallow to set at room temperature for at least 3 hours or, even better, overnight. The marshmallow will be too sticky and soft to cut if you try too soon.

8. Sprinkle a work surface or cutting board with the icing sugar. Run a knife along the top edge of the pan to loosen the marsh-mallow slab. Invert the pan and flip the marshmallow out onto the counter or board. Scoop up handfuls of the icing sugar and rub all over the marshmallow slab.

9. Use a large knife to cut the slab into 1- × 1-inch squares. Roll each of the freshly cut marshmallow squares in the remaining icing sugar to coat them completely.

If you—and most of your kitchen—are speckled with marshmallow by the time you finish this recipe, fear not! It's mostly sugar, so a little hot water and elbow grease will have things as good as new in no time.

Marshmallow Variations

TOASTED COCONUT MARSHMALLOWS

My personal favorite! Just substitute the 3 cups icing sugar with 3 cups unsweetened shredded coconut. To prepare the coconut: Preheat the oven to 325°F. Sprinkle the coconut onto a cookie sheet in one even layer and bake in the preheated oven for 15 minutes, until the coconut is a lovely golden brown, stirring every 5 minutes to make sure it toasts evenly. Remove from the oven and allow to cool. Follow Steps 8 and 9 to coat the marshmallows completely in toasted coconut.

RASPBERRY MARSHMALLOWS

In a small saucepan over medium heat, warm ¼ cup raspberry jam (any variety will do) until it becomes runny, about 3 minutes. Remove from the heat. Place a fine sieve over a small bowl and pour the warm jam through the sieve to catch any seeds and create a puree. Add the puree and one drop of red food coloring at Step 4 of the recipe.

MINT MARSHMALLOWS

These are fantastic in hot chocolate! Add 1 teaspoon of mint extract and 1 drop of green food coloring at Step 4 of the recipe. Make sure you do this at the end of the whisking process—if you add it too early it prevents the marshmallow from achieving its proper volume.

COFFEE MARSHMALLOWS

Add ½ cup of strongly brewed coffee or espresso instead of the water in Step 1, and add another ½ cup instead of the water in Step 2.

CINNAMON MARSHMALLOWS

 Another yummy option for your hot chocolate or, even better, melted on top of your sweet potatoes at Thanksgiving. Add 2 teaspoons of ground cinnamon at Step 4.

You can store your marshmallows in an airtight container, a re-sealable plastic bag or tightly wrapped in plastic wrap. You can also package them up in little cello bags as we do at the bakery and hand them out to family and friends for a yummy treat.

Top shelf

Butter BAKED GOODS

The
Mocha
S'More

4321 Dunbar Street
Vancouver BC
604 221 4333
butterbakedgoods.com

Butter BAKED GOODS

The
Homemade
S'more

4321 Dunbar Street
Vancouver BC
604 221 4333
butterbakedgoods.com

Butter BAKED GOODS

Chocolate
Toasted Coconut
Marshmallow

4321 Dunbar Street
Vancouver BC
604 221 4333
butterbakedgoods.com

Butter BAKED GOODS

Raspberry
White Chocolate
Marshmallow

4321 Dunbar Street
Vancouver BC
604 221 4333
butterbakedgoods.com

Bottom shelf

Butter BAKED GOODS

Toasted
Coconut
Marshmallow

4321 Dunbar Street
Vancouver BC
604 221 4333
butterbakedgoods.com

Butter BAKED GOODS

Strawberry
Marshmallow

4321 Dunbar Street
Vancouver BC
604 221 4333
butterbakedgoods.com

Butter BAKED GOODS

Pistachio
Marshmallow

4321 Dunbar Street
Vancouver BC
604 221 4333
butterbakedgoods.com

Butter BAKED GOODS

Coffee
Marshmallow

4321 Dunbar Street
Vancouver BC
604 221 4333
butterbakedgoods.com

Butter BAKED GOODS

Lemon
Marshmallow

4321 Dunbar Street
Vancouver BC
604 221 4333
butterbakedgoods.com

*T*his is a treat my young friend Kate introduced me to. The original version used Kraft marshmallows and melted Mackintosh's Toffee, and it really was delicious. Our Butter version has a few more steps involved, but I think the end result is worth the effort. We had great fun coming up with different riffs on the classic combination. To date my favorite is a banana marshmallow rolled in peanut butter and Rice Krispies, then dipped in milk chocolate—proving once again that you are only ever limited by your imagination.

Grenades

½ batch Butter's Famous
    Marshmallows (page 227)

4 cups Rice Krispies

2 cups heavy cream

½ cup whole milk

1 ½ cups granulated sugar

1 ½ cups dark brown sugar

1 teaspoon salt

3 tablespoons butter

½ cup light corn syrup

¼ cup water

2 pounds dark chocolate
    (about 4 cups chocolate chips)

MAKES: About 24 to 30 grenades

YOU WILL NEED: candy thermom-
    eter, cookie sheet lined with
    parchment paper

BEFORE YOU BEGIN: Prepare a batch of Butter's Famous Marshmallows (page 227). You only need half the batch so will have lots left over.

1. Place the Rice Krispies in a small bowl and set aside.

2. In a large saucepan over medium heat, combine the cream, milk, both sugars, salt, butter, corn syrup and water. Clip the candy thermometer to the side of the saucepan to monitor the temperature. Use a whisk to stir the caramel mixture constantly until it reaches 220°F. Remove from the heat and allow to cool for 1 minute (don't wait too long or the caramel will start to firm up.)

3. Use a fork to dip each marshmallow into the caramel mixture and gently move it around to coat the whole surface. Lightly tap the fork on the side of the bowl to remove any excess .

4. Immediately drop the marshmallows into the Rice Krispies and roll them around until completely coated. Place on the prepared cookie sheet.

5. Follow the steps on page 234 to temper the dark chocolate.

6. Use a fork to dip each marshmallow in the tempered chocolate. Lightly tap the fork on the edge of the bowl to help remove any excess. Place back on the cookie sheet, lined with fresh parchment paper.

7. Allow the chocolate to set for at least 1 hour before you enjoy (or place in the refrigerator to speed things up).

Make sure you roll all the marshmallows in both the caramel and the Rice Krispies before you temper the chocolate. It gets a little complicated to try to do all the steps at once, and your chocolate may lose temper if it sits too long. The grenades will keep in an airtight container for up to 2 weeks or in the freezer for several months.

*T*empering chocolate is a tricky process to master, but it's important if you want to be known for your amazing Kitchen Sink Bark or PB & J Cups! I think fireworks went off in the bakery the day I mastered it—or maybe they were just in my head. Regardless, it was a satisfying day. Be sure to have a little extra chocolate on hand the first few times you attempt it, just in case things don't quite go according to plan.*

Let's Talk Tempering

2 pound block of good quality milk or dark chocolate (about 4 cups chocolate chips). Plus an extra 1 pound (about 2 cups) just in case*

YOU WILL NEED: chocolate thermometer

Use a heatproof rubber spatula to scrape the sides of the bowl several times while the chocolate is melting to capture all the bits of chocolate.

1. In the bowl of a double boiler, or in a heatproof bowl set over a saucepan of simmering water, place two-thirds of the chocolate (make sure that the bottom of the bowl doesn't touch the water). Place the chocolate thermometer in the center and melt until it reads 115°F (dark chocolate) or 110°F (milk chocolate).

2. Remove from the heat and wipe the steam from the bottom of the bowl with a dry cloth to make sure that no water gets in the chocolate (this will cause the chocolate to seize and ruin the batch). Add the remaining "seed" chocolate and stir until melted and the overall temperature is 88-89°F (dark chocolate), or 84-86°F (milk chocolate). To bring the temperature down, place the bowl on a bag of frozen fruit or vegetables.

3. Test the chocolate for temper: Dip the back of a spoon into the chocolate then set it on the counter or on a piece of paper towel. If tempered properly, it should begin to set within a few minutes and have a satin finish. If it is dull and streaked, it has not reached temper yet. If this is the case, start the process over from Step 1: Heat the same chocolate again, and this time use the "just in case" chocolate as the "seed."

4. Once successfully tempered, begin to work with the chocolate as directed in the recipe. If it starts to set as you are working, place the bowl over simmering water again until the chocolate returns to tempering temperature (88-89°F for dark chocolate or 84-86°F for milk). Don't let the temperature rise above 90°F or it will fall out of temper again.

WHAT IS TEMPERING?

The tempering process produces a shiny chocolate with a good snap, the kind of snap you get when you break a chocolate bar. Think of the shininess and snap of chocolate as its memory; when chocolate is melted it loses its memory. That's why if you simply melt chocolate and then dip something into it—a strawberry, say—it never really sets firm again unless it's refrigerated. Adding a little tempered chocolate (a process called seeding) to the melted chocolate helps remind it what it used to be and gives it something to build on to regain its shininess and snap.

*F*or some, the s'more is all about camping and the great outdoors. For me, it's all about chocolate, graham crackers and marshmallow. This version can be made, assembled and enjoyed in the safety of your own home—or you can risk being eaten by a bear by taking the various homemade elements with you on your next camping trip. Toast the marshmallows carefully over an open fire as they are a little more fragile than regular store-bought ones.

The Homemade S'more

Butter's Own Graham Crackers
(page 87)

12 x large Butter's Famous
Marshmallows (page 227)

2 cups dark chocolate chips

MAKES: **12 s'mores**

YOU WILL NEED: **cookie sheet**

If you choose to go the camping route, you need to pack: a container of homemade graham crackers, a re-sealable plastic bag of homemade marshmallows and a couple of bars of really good chocolate.

BEFORE YOU BEGIN: **Prepare a batch of Butter's Own Graham Crackers (page 87) and a batch of Butter's Famous Marshmallows (page 227), cut into 2- × 2-inch squares. You only need 12 large marshmallows so will have lots left over.**

1. Place the marshmallows in a large sieve and give them a good shake to remove any excess icing sugar.

2. In a small saucepan over medium heat, melt the chocolate until shiny and smooth (or melt in the microwave for about 30 seconds on high).

3. Spoon 1 tablespoon of melted chocolate onto the wrong side of a graham cracker and top with 1 marshmallow.

The wrong side of the cracker is the bottom side, the one that was sitting on the cookie sheet. The top side is the right side. Seems unfair, I know, but I didn't make the rules. Clearly some cookie from the right side did.

4. Spoon 1 tablespoon of chocolate onto the wrong side of another graham cracker and place it (chocolate side down) on top of the marshmallow. Press down lightly on the cracker to sandwich together.

5. Allow the chocolate to set for at least 1 hour before you enjoy (or place in the refrigerator to speed things up).

*T*his is a fun treat to bring out your inner artist. Throwing chocolate around with total abandon will always guarantee a good time, and the best part is that you get to snack on your masterpiece when you're done.

Jackson Pollock Popcorn

2 large bags microwave popcorn
(makes about 24 cups)

½ cup butter

1 cup dark brown sugar

¼ cup light corn syrup

1 teaspoon salt

1 teaspoon pure vanilla

¼ teaspoon baking soda

½ cup white chocolate

½ cup dark chocolate

MAKES: **About 15 bags of popcorn**

YOU WILL NEED: **2 cookie sheets
lined with parchment paper**

You can store the popcorn in an airtight container for up to 1 week. Or you could portion it into cello bags tied with ribbon, and gift them to friends the next time you see a movie together.

1. Preheat the oven to 250°F.

2. Follow the instructions to prepare the microwave popcorn and place in a very large bowl. Set aside.

3. In a medium saucepan over medium heat, melt the butter. Add the sugar, corn syrup and salt. Bring to a boil, stirring constantly. Stop stirring when the mixture starts to boil, and then boil for 5 minutes.

4. Remove from the heat and stir in the vanilla and baking soda to create the caramel.

5. Pour the hot caramel over the popcorn and use two large spoons to toss the popcorn (as if you were tossing a salad) and evenly coat the kernels with caramel. Spread the popcorn evenly across the prepared cookie sheets.

6. Bake in the preheated oven for 45 minutes. Toss the popcorn again every 15 minutes to ensure even baking.

7. Remove from the oven and allow to cool on the cookie sheets.

8. Meanwhile, use two separate double boilers, or two small bowls placed over two pots of simmering water, to melt the white chocolate and dark chocolate separately. Use a large spoon to drizzle the melted chocolates randomly over the popcorn (with great artistic flair!).

9. Allow the chocolate to set for at least 1 hour. Then break the popcorn into bite-sized chunks.

*T*his is always great fun to make at the bakery, as it is a little different every time. It all depends on what we have on hand. You can put everything but the kitchen sink into this bark, but just make sure to include both some chewy things and some crunchy things. The rest is up to you!

Kitchen Sink Bark

2 pounds dark chocolate
(about 4 cups chocolate chips)

3 cups in total of various goodies,
broken into bite-size pieces.
Options include:
M&Ms
potato chips
pretzels
gummy bears
gum drops
marshmallows
nuts (peanuts, pecans or
almonds)
dried fruit (cherries, pineapple
or apricots)
shredded coconut
licorice nibs
Oreo cookies

MAKES: **About 12 good-sized pieces**

YOU WILL NEED: **cookie sheet lined
with parchment paper**

1. Follow the steps on page 234 to temper the chocolate.

2. Fold two-thirds of your chosen goodies into the chocolate and mix gently to incorporate.

3. Spread the chocolate mixture onto the prepared cookie sheet. Sprinkle the remaining goodies over the bark.

> The mixture may be a little thick (depending on your chosen ingredients) so don't be afraid to get messy by pressing the bark down with the palm of your hands. The goodies should be partially submerged in the chocolate so they don't pop off once the chocolate has hardened.

4. Allow the mixture to set for at least 1 hour (or place it in the refrigerator to speed up the process). Once set, snap it off into random-sized pieces, approximately 3 × 3 inches each.

> If the chocolate has been tempered properly, the bark will keep in an airtight container for several weeks. It makes a fantastic gift, packaged in tins or cello bags, for friends and family.

As a kid, Reese's Peanut Butter Cups were one of my favorite things. I'm pretty sure that even from a young age I was already planning on ways that I could improve the original recipe. Thirty-plus years later and I think I've managed to do just that. For me, using a really good dark chocolate elevates this recipe beyond a corner-store treat, especially when I use a really good raspberry jam. I find the best jams at my local farmers' market. Small-batch jams using loads of quality fruit always taste more delicious than something from the grocery store shelf.

Peanut Butter and Jam Cups

Peanut Butter Butter Cream
    (page 135)

2 pounds dark chocolate
    (about 4 cups chocolate chips)

½ cup really good raspberry jam

1 cup white chocolate chips

1 drop red food coloring

12 salted peanuts, shelled and
    halved

MAKES: 24 PB&J Cups

YOU WILL NEED: 2 mini muffin pans
    lined with mini paper liners,
    small piping bag fitted with a
    small round tip

BEFORE YOU BEGIN: Prepare a batch of Peanut Butter Butter Cream (page 135)

1. Follow the steps on page 234 to temper the dark chocolate.

2. Fill each paper liner half full with the tempered chocolate. Use the piping bag to carefully pipe the top of the chocolate with Peanut Butter Butter Cream, about ¹/₂ teaspoon on each, then top with ¹/₂ teaspoon of raspberry jam. Fill the balance of the paper cups with more tempered chocolate. Tap the muffin pans lightly on the countertop to settle the mixture and smooth the tops of the cups.

3. In a small saucepan over low heat, melt the white chocolate (or melt in the microwave for about 30 seconds on high). Add the red food coloring to the melted chocolate to tint it a light pink.

4. Use a small spoon to place a small drop of the white chocolate on the center of each chocolate cup, and top with one peanut half.

5. Allow the chocolate cups to set for at least 2 hours (or place in the refrigerator to speed up the process).

Once the chocolate has set, the PB&J cups will keep in an airtight container for up to 1 week.

*This treat falls under the category I like to call "A little something, something."
They are the perfect little pick-me-up around three in the afternoon, or a simple
way to finish dinner with friends. Just a little something, something to enjoy.*

Peanut Butter Balls

½ cup butter, room temperature

1 cup peanut butter, smooth or
    crunchy

2 cups icing sugar, sifted

1 cup graham crumbs

3 cups dark chocolate chips

2 cups peanuts

MAKES: **About 48 balls**

YOU WILL NEED: **cookie sheet lined
with parchment paper, small ice
cream scoop**

1. In a stand mixer fitted with a paddle attachment, cream the butter and peanut butter on medium to high speed until light and fluffy. Scrape down the sides of the bowl.

2. Turn the mixer to low and add the icing sugar and graham crumbs and mix until well combined. The dough should pull off the sides of the bowl and come together.

3. Use the ice cream scoop to drop 48 equally sized portions of dough onto the prepared cookie sheet. Roll each portion between your palms to create a little round ball. Place the balls back on the cookie sheet once formed.

4. Refrigerate or freeze for about 1 hour, until cold and firm (this will make them easy to dip and roll later).

5. Use a large knife or a food processor to chop the peanuts until very fine, then transfer to a small bowl.

If you are using a food processor, be careful to not look away as it only takes a minute to go too far and find you've made yourself peanut butter!

6. In a double boiler, or in a heatproof bowl set over a saucepan of simmering water, melt the chocolate chips until smooth and shiny.

7. Use a fork to dip each peanut butter ball into the melted chocolate and roll it around to coat the whole surface. Lightly tap the fork on the side of the bowl to remove any excess. You may need to re-warm the chocolate if it starts to thicken up as it cools.

8. Drop the balls into the chopped peanuts and roll around until completely coated. Then roll each ball between your palms to help the peanuts adhere. Place back on the cookie sheet.

9. Allow to set in the refrigerator for 30 minutes before serving.

These balls will keep in an airtight container in the refrigerator for several weeks or in the freezer for several months.

*W*e started making this brittle at the request of my best friend, Jan. Actually, it wasn't so much a request as a direct order. She knew what she was talking about because it has proven to be crazy popular. It's a sure way to impress your friends, as no one seems to be able to figure out how all the bubbles get in there.

Chocolate Honeycomb Brittle

1 ½ cups granulated sugar

¼ cup dark corn syrup

¼ cup water

1 tablespoon honey

1 tablespoon baking soda

2 pounds dark chocolate
(about 4 cups chocolate chips)

MAKES: **About 12 to 16 pieces**

YOU WILL NEED: **cookie sheet lined with parchment paper, candy thermometer**

1. In a medium saucepan over medium-high heat, combine the sugar, corn syrup, water and honey. Bring to a boil, stirring constantly. Clip a candy thermometer to the side of the saucepan and reduce the heat so the mixture is at a low boil. Do not stir but maintain the low boil until the temperature reaches 300°F, then remove from the heat.

2. Gently sift the baking soda over the brittle mixture and use a heatproof spatula to stir it in. When the brittle has almost stopped bubbling, gently pour it onto the prepared cookie sheet. This process (from when you add the baking soda) takes only a minute, so be prepared to work quickly.

3. Allow the brittle to cool on the cookie sheet until it has set, about 5 minutes. Break into random-sized pieces.

4. Follow the steps on page 234 to temper the chocolate.

5. Use a fork to dip each piece of brittle into the chocolate. Lightly tap the fork on the edge of the saucepan to remove any excess. Use a small knife to push the brittle off the fork and onto the cookie sheet, lined with a fresh sheet of parchment paper.

6. Allow the chocolate to set for at least 1 hour (or place in the refrigerator for 10 minutes to speed things up).

The brittle will keep in an airtight container for up to 1 week.

*S*ometimes you start out in one direction, then life throws you a curveball and you find yourself headed in another. Like my plan to have a little bakery on the west side of Vancouver, and the next thing you know, I'm building a marshmallow factory. Sometimes those little twists and turns can turn out to be the best thing. Like the day we set out to make our salted caramels. Just for a change we decided to add some chocolate and espresso powder to create a mocha caramel. Surprise . . . we got mocha fudge! You've got to go where the universe directs you, and clearly it wanted us to make some delicious fudge.

Surprise Mocha Fudge

2 tablespoons instant espresso powder

2 tablespoons hot water

2 cups heavy cream

½ cup whole milk

½ cup light corn syrup

¼ cup water

3 tablespoons butter

1 ½ cups granulated sugar

1 ½ cups dark brown sugar

1 teaspoon salt

½ cup dark chocolate chips

MAKES: **64 pieces**

YOU WILL NEED: **(9- × 13-inch) baking pan buttered and lined with parchment paper (see page 30), candy thermometer**

1. In a small bowl, dissolve the espresso powder in the hot water. Set aside.

2. In a large saucepan over medium heat, combine the cream, milk, corn syrup, water, butter, both sugars and salt. Clip a candy thermometer to the side of the saucepan. Use a whisk to stir the mixture constantly until the temperature reaches 250°F. Remove from the heat.

3. Add the chocolate chips and espresso to create a hot fudge. Whisk to combine. Pour the hot fudge into the prepared baking pan. Use a spatula to scrape down the sides of the saucepan and spread the fudge evenly across the pan. It doesn't take long for the fudge to start to set, so work quickly but carefully.

5. Allow the fudge to cool and set completely, about 45 minutes.

6. Run a small knife along the two edges of the pan that do not have parchment handles. Carefully remove the slab from the pan. Cut the fudge into eight even squares, and then cut each square into eight even pieces, to create 64 individual-sized pieces, about 1 × 1 ¹/₂ inches each.

If you wrap each piece of fudge individually in a small piece of parchment paper or waxed paper, they all can be stored in an airtight container for up to 2 weeks.

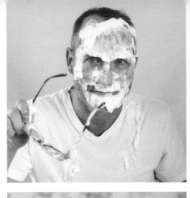

Where the heck do I begin to say thank you to all the wonderful people who have helped make this book a reality? At the beginning, I guess.

Thanks to Mum and Dad. Without your hard work, I quite literally wouldn't be here. Your support and encouragement over the years have made all the difference, as did letting me make a mess in the kitchen when I was little.

To my sister, Pixie, the first person who didn't think my idea of opening a bakery was crazy (or if she did, then for having the best poker face ever).

To everyone who has come to work at Butter over the years. Sometimes it works and sometimes it doesn't, but we no doubt had a few laughs along the way.

To Kazuko, my right-hand woman from the beginning. You make it all possible. It's funny to think that it all started with a little bow.

To Trish, the best-looking farm girl you ever did meet and Butter's reigning cupcake queen. Thank you for being there.

To Tomo, the man of a thousand skills. You make me smile and wish I drank coffee.

To Naomi and Naoe. You make all things marshmallow possible, and for this I will be forever grateful. Did you ever imagine you would one day manage a marshmallow factory?

To Maggie, Satomi, Maria, Hiromi, Mango, Cody, Liam, Heather and the rest of the Butter family. I couldn't ask for a better team.

To Don the Milkman, without whom there would be no butter for Butter. In rain, sleet, snow or sun, you always deliver.

To all of our wonderful customers, you are the very reason Butter exists. Thank you, thank you, thank you for all your support!

To our friends the "Buttersons" and the Murphys. You make this world, and most importantly my world, a better place. I plan to feed you baked goods for a long, long time to come.

To my best friend, Janya. Everyone should be lucky enough to have a Jan in their life. But not this one. She's mine. I know we will be talking, walking and playing Scrabble until the end of time.

To Janis, the most talented photographer I have ever met and an all-round lovely person. This book would not be what it is without you, and working with you on it has been a true honor. Thanks for making all my baked goods look so darn good!

To Kelly Hill. Thank you for all your hard work and endless talent. You have done an amazing job in designing a book that really reflects all that Butter is.

To Robert and Lindsay at Appetite. Thank you for taking my call that fateful day. You really are the best! I hope we get to make many more books together.

To India. You are everything to me, and so much more. You're the reason I do what I do. If I've made you proud, then I've done my job.

To Paul, the half that makes me whole. I wouldn't want to be me without you. Thank you for always being there, listening to me, being so damn smart (as maddening as that is!), eating all my baking and making me laugh. I love you. *B*

INDEX

NOTE: Page numbers in italics refer to photographs.